T0148343

Boston Tea Party: PHASE II

John Doe

iUniverse, Inc.
New York   Bloomington

Boston Tea Party: PHASE II

iUniverse books may be ordered through booksellers or by contacting:

iUniverse
1663 Liberty Drive
Bloomington, IN 47403
www.iuniverse.com
1-800-Authors (1-800-288-4677)

ISBN: 978-1-4502-2189-4 (pbk)
ISBN: 978-1-4502-2190-0 (ebk)

Printed in the United States of America
iUniverse rev. date: 4/16/10

About the Author

Because I live in a predominantly Democratic State, I am using the pen name of John Doe to write this book. As you might understand, I do not want any repercussions for writing a conservative book to affect my kids at school or family in general. The name selection, John Doe, is based on an old movie where there was a man who was found with amnesia and could not remember his name. Akin my chosen pen name, I do not recall the name of the movie but Edward G. Robinson, Barbara Stanwick and I think Alan Paige were the stars. As the star of the movie was recovering in the hospital, they called him John Doe. As the movie progresses, the politicians turned this man into a hero, and as long as he did what they wanted him to do he was a hero. As soon as he wouldn't do what they wanted him to do, he was a problem that they had to get rid of. Due to his moral character, they decided to destroy him. It was a unique movie, but I personally do not want to be the hero nor do I want to be the problem. Let's just go with a name for self preservation for now.

I grew up in a small town in Minnesota. My parents were of German and Swedish heritage on my father's side and Polish heritage on my mother's side. I grew up as a Roman Catholic, and I am one of the Knights of Columbus (the Knights of Columbus, if you are not familiar with them, do fund raisers for catholic charities like the funding for men to become priests and money for pro-life agencies, and many other charities). My education status is an AAS in the liberal arts. I am a home owner, and a tax payer. I am retired from the AF Reserve and spent well over ten years in the active Army.

From my military back ground you can easily assume that I love our country. Fortunately, I have never had to go to war, but I was on an airfield once waiting to be dropped in to a conflict, it was so close that we had live ammo already loaded, but it was canceled at the last moment. I was also in the Army on active duty at the tail end of Vietnam, during the Panama City Invasion, during the Faulken Islands crisis, during Somalia, during Dessert Storm and during Dessert Shield. So I could have been sent to war many times over.

Thank you for reading this book. I appreciate the time you have taken out of your busy life to read about my views and concerns for our country.

Sincerely,

John Doe

Dedication

This Book is dedicated to the Americans who are concerned, frustrated, and even afraid of the way our government is moving. While I listened to the radio one evening, a woman on the Rush Limbaugh show, almost in tears about how this country is becoming a socialist country, showed her frustrations and like mindedness. Her emotions and concerns inspired me. Before I heard this woman's remarks, I had experienced some of the same emotions. I was actually considering moving to Canada. Naturally, that doesn't really fix this problem because Canada also has a socialist medical program!

So I thought there must be something <u>we can do now</u> . We can not wait until the 2010 elections. As well, it is time for me to act. I am writing this book with ideas to counter this new and subversive socialism and calling my first book "The Boston Tea Party, Phase II".

I propose that the way; we the people start fighting back now is by the use of embargos much like the civil revolt against British oppression at the original Boston Tea Party.

Remarkably, the membership at the TEA PARTY movement are not even recognized by the mass media, not even the 9-12 movement on Washington that I heard had 1.8 million people in attendance. The tea parties were started by people upset with this administration, and the idea of them raising taxes. The 9-12 movement on Washington D.C. was a march that was this group's push to be noticed. This was not covered by the mass media, when the Ramadan prayer day was covered and I heard they only had about ½ million people. The women could not even pray with the men, but that part of the Ramadan prayer day was not covered.

If all of the conservatives will follow my proposed list of embargos, we can tell this administration a great deal. We the people can show this administration that we can vote now without waiting until 2010 to vote and by taking action. Our voices will be heard even without Mass Media Coverage! One of President Obama's own themes: the redistribution of wealth: can be used to have our voices heard. The greatest threat is when we the conservatives in great numbers <u>do not do</u> something. When we stand idly by, the liberal's agenda is free to move its will against our countries best interest. My embargo strategy also includes measures for the redistribution of wealth contrary to the intentions of Democrats. In participating with my embargo concepts, this redistribution of wealth strategy can happen. By participating in these embargos I will show you redistribution of wealth.

The theme "redistribution of wealth" is perfect for the voting without waiting to vote movement. What we need to do is to simply hit these socialists were it really matters, in their pocket books! As you read on you will see how and what we can do.

As well, I am also dedicating this book to Fox News and the talk show hosts for standing up in the face of this administration in what Fox News believes is the truth, which is also many Americans beliefs, as well as my own beliefs. These talk show hosts take a great deal of rhetoric from people for what they say and what they really believe.

This book is about fighting back now, and what we the people can do, to counter this communist/ socialist administration. I believe that the use of these embargo techniques can show the radically liberal part of the Democratic Party that we will not wait until 2010 to vote and do something about these socialist agendas now. It is the Liberal part of the Democratic Party that needs to be shown that we do have power even though they have control of congress for now.

Now, more than ever, I believe many people are feeling the same way I did when I was listening to the concerns of the woman on the Rush Limbaugh show. So if we all band together there is something we can all do, now. We must unite and take action.

Introduction

This is a "how to" book, about how to fight against these liberal agendas. My goal is to embargo the liberals. For quick use of this book, read Chapter I, then read the quick list of hard choices or Embargos. Appendix A and then read the book conclusion. By doing it this way you can very quickly start to apply this principles and strategies of this book. Acting quickly and effectively is important.

By following the recipe of my embargos plan, I believe we can take action quickly. We are in charge not the liberals because we are the majority and we are going to take our country back as much as we can until we can vote the liberals out of office in 2010. I have an idea as to what I believe the President's dream is. Then by reading the book conclusion you will get a brief description of what is in each chapter.

There are 13 Embargos in this book. You may not be able to do all of them, because of your job. That's alright; just do as many embargos as you can. We need each others help to be noticed, because this administration has the mass media in their back pocket and have drawn a line in the sand. Just by not covering our Tea Parties and the march on Washington. So now they will have to deal with our embargos. The thing is if we can get more and more Americans to start following these embargos week after week until the election of 2010 these embargos will make the Liberals take notice. The administration has said that it is going to subsidize the news paper industry. To what point is their value in trying to save an industries death due to a radical change in technology and how people read the news? With what we do it will be even harder to save the papers, we can make a difference and let business take its course.

In Chapter I, I will explain what I believe the vision of Barrack Obama is, and in the rest of the book I will explain what we the people can do now and not feel so helpless. Also why Barrack Obama appears to be doing so many strange things! Almost like he is still campaigning and didn't win the election.

As well, I will cover these issues:

- Why after winning the Presidential Election and becoming the most powerful man on the earth, does he travel the world on what the conservatives call his Apology Tour?
- Why push a stimulus package that is all pork and almost NO JOBS, when our country needs jobs?
- Why is there such a push to pass a medical bill to have the state control 1/6th of our economy, when in reality we need a medical insurance overhaul not a health care overhaul that is run by the government? When our health care is the best in the world.

- Why some say there are signs that Hillary may be getting ready to throw her hat in the Presidential race again? Does she know something we don't!
- Why do some say that the Presidents speeches are like he is still campaigning?
- Why did Obama win the Nobel Prize? Having his name submitted after being in office less than 2 weeks and winning it for the statement, "we will reach out our hand if you will only unclench your fist"! Saying this while his country is at War in 2 different countries and many others are seemingly more deserving of this award and while we are at war with terrorism (Man Made Disasters.)
- Why is there such a push to pass cap and trade?
- Why there is serious talk about being taxed for a carbon footprint?
- Why are all of these 3rd world countries praising Barrack Obama, like he is a rock star not the leader of America? After all we are a major country in the world that believes in capitalism and not socialism. So do they know something we don't!

Why do these things seem so odd and bother us so much. There is a simple answer. When you go through Officer training for the military you learn that a lie of omission is still a lie. A lawyer would argue this point. I understand that our President is a lawyer, and we the people believe that something has been omitted!

This book was written to be a tool to for the conservatives of this country to band together to fight liberalism without waiting until 2010 and 2012 to vote them out of office.

We must have our voices heard. A new Cold War has begun.

Contents

Chapter I
The True Situation!

Socialism will truly bring us out of a recession. Hitler took his broken little country and turned it into a world power in 2 short years. Yes in 2 short years, because in Socialism the people get very little and the government gets the rest, and the government decides what the rest is. The elite powerful people became stronger and more powerful. As Hitler's lower class grew larger and poorer. In fact the lower class became even poorer than before Hitler took it over, because he put that extra money in his Army.

However; socialism does not motivate people to work harder, instead they work harder to get out of work because the work ethic declines because you make the same pay and benefits whether your work is sloppy, or your work is superb. On this note, there are really smart doctors, there are smart doctors, and there are not so smart doctors. After this Health Care bill is passed and all the doctors make the same amount of money. Do you think they will still be running test groups to see how a drug or a procedure works? Why would doctors do this, if they get no compensation or are not getting recognition for their research? So there will be no medical advances or very few medical advances, because the doctors will be receiving no extra compensation.

You may not believe this, but my belief is that if it walks like a duck and it quacks like a duck it is a duck. My analogy is; if you get paid from the state to be unemployed and your health care is provided for by the state, it is socialism. When you get something for free it really isn't free, in fact this will actually cost you your freedoms. The other freedom truth is that freedom isn't free.

Why is this freedom issue so important? Our country was founded on having personal freedoms, especially freedom of religion. People flocked to this nation because of our freedoms. Now freedom is vital because if I am correct about what Barrack Obama's vision is, the average American will lose a lot of his/her freedoms. Take the Catholic religion, Catholics believe in the family: being a man and a woman and the number of children that they want. Not the number of children the state wants them to have or tax them for each person over that amount in their family (or a Carbon Footprint *1). This freedom may be lost just like China is restricting the number of children you have or taxing you for your children. This maybe a good thing, because it might make us Americans wake up and <u>not</u> take our freedoms for granted. We might start to see them as a rights and not a privilege and then maybe we will fight for them. The problem is that this Administration maybe taking some of our major freedoms and Americans need to stand up to this Administration. As we use these embargos we will be standing up to this Administration, Thank God.

Back to the situation at hand, we have a president that has done some unprecedented things, with some question as to why he is doing some of these things. I will tell you some of the things that seem unprecedented and then I will tell you why I think this Administration is doing these unprecedented things. I will also tell you what I think we can do about these things now!

- Why after winning the presidency and becoming the most powerful man on the earth, does he travel the earth on what the conservatives call his Apology tour!
- Why push a stimulus package that is all pork and almost no jobs, when our country needs jobs.
- Why is there such a push to pass a Health Care Bill to have the state control 1/6th of our economy, when in reality we need a medical insurance overhaul?
- Why do some people say there are signs that Hillary maybe getting ready to throw her hat in the presidential race again? Does she know something we do not know?
- Why do some people say that the Presidents speeches are like he is still campaigning?
- Why does Barrack Obama's name get submitted for the Nobel Peace Prize and win it after being in office less then 2 weeks; for the statement "we will reach out our hand if you will only unclench your fist"? Saying this while his country is at war in 2 different countries and at war with terrorism. Not to mention that many other people who really deserved this award were nominated and not picked!
- Why is there such a push to pass cap and Trade?

- Why is there all of this serious talk about being taxed for a carbon footprint (a human exhaling carbon dioxide)?
- Lastly, why are so many of these 3rd world communist countries praising Barrack Obama, like he is a rock star and not the leader of a major Capitalistic Country? Do they know something we do not?

Before I can tell you what I believe this Administrations real agenda is I must tell you that there are under tones in the world moving toward a world government. This is going through many of our colleges, because most colleges have a liberal spin on life. There is a world government coming, and the day for a decision is near. This type of premise is great for Star Trek the TV series, but we as a nation with a successful free market system and the highest economic level in the world; will be hurt with a world government, we are not ready for this. We will hurt financially and some of our freedoms our in jeopardy.

This world Government is made in the disguise of being a green treaty for our planet, and it is getting its start in Copenhagen Norway as the climate change treaty. This New World Order will probably be headquartered with the United Nations, or in Norway, they will say many things like the United Nations does, but taking very little action like the United Nations, and when they do take action they will be expecting America to lead the way like with this climate change stuff.

Now the answers to these questions as I promised you and what I believe the Presidents secret agenda is. I believe that Barrack Obama plans to move from president of the United States to Emperor of the world. Now if he does become Emperor of the world you can see how each of those earlier statements fit into place.

- Why after winning the presidency and becoming the most powerful man on the earth, does he travel the earth on what the conservatives call his Apology tour! *He is planning a bigger office. He is running for the office of Emperor of the World on American Taxes!*
- Why push a stimulus package that is all pork and almost no jobs, when our country needs jobs. *He wants to keep the America economy down, so that in his campaign for Emperor so he can show how he made American bow down to Socialism and show the world how it works.*
- Why is there such a push to pass a Health Care Bill to have the state control 1/6th of our economy, when in reality we need a Medical insurance overhaul? *During his world Campaign he will be able to say I gave America a government run medical care program and now I will do that for the World.*
- Why some people say there are signs that Hillary maybe getting ready to throw her hat in the presidential race again? Does she know something we do not know? *I believe that many of the Democrats in congress are aware of this world government movement and maybe even that our president maybe in the running for Emperor of the World. Maybe that was why he did not seem depressed about possibility of being a one term Presidentr.*

- Why do some say that the Presidents speeches are like he is still campaigning? *This one is simple, he is still campaigning.*

- Why does Barrack Obama's name get submitted for the Nobel Peace Prize and win it after being in office less then 2 weeks for the statement "we will reach out our hand if you will only unclench your fist"? Saying this while his country is at war in 2 different countries and at war with terrorism. Not to mention that many other people who really deserved this award were nominated and were not picked! *Much of the world is aware of his attempt to turn America into a socialist nation. If they were to see American turned into a socialist country he would be a shoe in for Emperor. It is a part of his personal beliefs for what it would take to become the Emperor of the World.*

- Why there is a push to pass cap and Trade? *This is another move to keep America down and show the world his ability to lead no matter how many are against him. You are probably thinking he will meet resistance. He believes he owns the mass media and that his popularity will not meet resistance no matter what he does. Do any of his left wing congressmen know of this?*

- Why is there all of this serious talk about being taxed for a carbon footprint (a human exhaling carbon dioxide)? *As a world government that will do very little of anything, this would be the only thing they could tax the world for that would make any sense. That is why they have to push so hard on this climate change agenda to make sense for what they are proposing. Only a small portion of*

> *this money would go to developing nations to help them stop pollution. It is an industry to support very little environment and the rest will go to the New World Order Government.*

- Lastly, why are so many of these 3rd world communist countries praising Barrack Obama, like he is a rock star and not the leader of a major Capitalistic Country? Do they know something we don't? *They know if the president of America can make America go along with this Carbon Footprint / Global Warming agenda the rest of the world will eventually follow. These Communist /socialist countries will get money out of America. The way Barrack Obama was trying to give $100 billion dollars of America's tax money to the new World Order for this Global Warming project in Copenhagen.*

We can stop this by following the fight back now techniques, using the embargo techniques explained in this book. Then later I will need your help again with your vote. We will also have to tell people what we know, because the state run media will not cover this. In fact fox news may not cover this because of the seriousness of these embargos. My idea of Barrack Obama's vision is an assumption, but one with well thought out conclusions. If we in America don't stop this world communism, no one country will be big enough to stop it later. Maybe Israel and Great Brittan together could because Israel and Great Brittan have enough power to sway other countries, but they will have to stand together. You see Russia or China will not be involved in paying money to some group of eggheads without any empirical data as proof, not with them using this made up data that they are using. I am sure Russia and China have their own records of temperatures that would not support these radical theories. I also believe that some of the far left Democratic congressmen; are aware of this movement; and they are for the New World Order.

I believe if enough Americans become aware of this movement we can stop it before it starts, but if we do nothing the New World Order will have the whole world run by way of communism. The world is also trying to get a world dollar, and this would destroy the United States economy as we know it. There is already a world health Organization. Next there will be the Hospital of the World, with all hospitals taking the new world dollars. We will be paying for our carbon footprints with this same new world order dollar. We will have to pay for carbon footprints when there is no proven scientific basis for this ridiculous concept? This is how the New World Order will control the world, with the same dollar paying all the bills.

Imagine America being the one of the rich countries that will eventually have to pay for many of the poor countries of the world. There is no telling how much tax we will have to pay to the New World Order government along with the state and federal taxes; I know <u>I cannot even afford a 10 percent increase in my taxes.</u>

This may scare you as much as it does me, but read on, because we the conservatives can change this, but we will need the help of both the Republican Conservatives as well as the Democratic Conservatives. I am going to be asking all of you to make some tough changes in your life.

I am making an Observation here;

- Bob the builder… Can we build it…Yes we can!
- Barrack Obama…Can we change… Yes we can!

This is scary that a President can use a preschooler's chant to make everyone love him, but Yes he can! When I was in the Army in Germany, I met a woman who was our teacher; she taught us simple things about Germany. Some basic German words and sentences and she took us on a tour downtown, to learn a little bit about the local history. One day 3 of us stayed after class and we where asking her some questions. Hitler came up and she told us that the German people loved Hitler. As a little girl she heard Hitler speak. She said he was a very charismatic speaker, all of the adults around her were cheering. After all Hitler brought the German people from a little broken down country to a world power. She said back then there was no mass media, so unless you were against the fatherland, you would not see the arrests and the seizing of property. The German people did not know he was executing people (the Jewish people in the ovens). Her family did not realize this until years later, and then she said they felt shame!

Another observation is that Hitler and President Obama are both charismatic speakers that mesmerize their audiences. Both of these men were and are captive speakers, take Obama's followers they see him as a man who can do no wrong. The average person does not believe in <u>everything</u> their president does but yet Obama's followers seem to agree with everything that this president says.

On the Fox News channel they often talk about 2 things this Administration said were important. One of the things is how this Administration said it was going to be more transparent then any other Administration. Yet before a key vote on their Health Care Bill, our president talks with congressmen behind closed doors. With doors closed showing no transparency we are left to imagine what happened behind those closed doors. The other thing that Fox news talks about is this Chicago style politics. With the thought of Chicago style politics, what are we supposed to think happened behind those closed doors? With these doors closed we the American people can believe anything that we want to.

We want to believe that these congressmen are offered things for their districts or political aid for their next campaign. This aid could come in the form of campaign money or visitation from the President of America.

Although after the campaigns in New Jersey and Virginia the association with the President doesn't seem to be any kind of advantage, and the offer of more campaign funds doesn't seem to be that big of an advantage either when the Democratic Party has out spent the Republican Party (Conservatives) 2 to 1 and in some cases the Democrats still lost.

So what else does the Administration have to offer these congressmen, they could offer them big money in their constituent's districts or maybe even federal jobs in their districts. With Chicago style politics it is possible that something else was offered behind those closed doors? Again because those doors are closed we can imagine anything we want.

These things that I have just explained to you may make you very anxious, and when I first figured out what I believe that Presidents ultimate goal might be "The Emperor of the New World Order", it terrified me, too. But you do not need to be terrified, because once you absorb this concept, you get really mad and then you need a way to defeat this socialism. So if you and most of the true Americans-Conservatives join me, we the people in this nation, can unite as the Tea Party Movement has already shown us and stand and defeat this radical socialist movement.

So read on, the next chapters will make you feel better because you will be doing something in a peaceful manner.

These chapters are very short and informative, and you will feel better after reading this short book.

Please help me take back our country: the country I love and know run by a republic not socialism. The techniques in this book that you may choose to follow are tough choices, but these tough choices you will be making are essential to take back America.

*1. Carbon footprint is the carbon dioxide that people, animals (pets or animals raised for food-cattle, sheep, pigs, chickens, and etcetera) and equipment like cars and trucks and tractors produce.

SUMMARY

In this chapter I explained what I believe our countries situation is, and how no major media televised the Tea Party Movements March on Washington that I heard was between 1.5 and 1.8 million people in strength per. I heard those estimates on the Fox network. Later in this book one of our embargos deals with the Mass media's coverage.

I also said the answers to defeat this movement are coming, and not to feel disheartened about the way this government is moving. Your voice will be heard if you make the tough choices and we stand together.

Chapter II
Socialism is the Problem

The first thing we need to do is to show the liberals in this country, that the dollar not the pen, is mightier than the sword. This is not illegal or immoral, but in fact it is an embargo. We want our voices heard in the *mainstream media*, so we organize and we march in a peaceful manner in large numbers and yet if you don't watch Fox News you *don't see any coverage.* The main stream media did not cover us, I feel myself to be a member of Tea Party movement even though I was not there, I am sorry for not being with you on the march on Washington, but everyone who feels affiliated to the Tea Party movement and who wanted to be there could not afford the trip. In this economy 1.8 million people is a large group and yet no main stream media coverage. It is ironic how the Strength in Numbers makes the Acronym of (SIN) especially since it was a sin by the mainstream media <u>not</u> to cover our march. We thought that the strength in Numbers would help us get news coverage, however it did not in this case, so we will have to find new ways to get noticed!

So now if we unite in other ways we will be heard, for example, by <u>not showing up & not spending our money in certain places,</u> we will be heard. We will create embargos against the liberal party that will let us be heard. I hope to have this book noticed by Fox News and at least have the contents get some national attention. I also hope the Tea Party members will read it and follow it, because I am calling it The Boston Tea Party, phase II, this book tells you how to <u>do something now</u> without having to wait until 2010 and 2012 elections to vote. It starts by using embargoing techniques as our way of voting without waiting to vote. The original tea party was about a revolution, of violently taking the tea with a tax that was believed to become a monopoly and throwing the tea in the bay, also causing a financial burden on the business men of England. Well I hope to cause a financial burden on the liberals, in a peaceful financial display against the liberals, without violence.

So in this phase II, *we will peacefully protest using our* <u>right to not spend money,</u> to get noticed. So Phase II is not using our money to protest this socialist way of life, and use embargos to protest bills with a socialist bias being forced down our throats. For years now when you try to discuss things with liberals they would throw up their arms and start to yell; when you don't see it there way, so instead of trying to continuing our discussions with them we are forced to walk away. Well we are fed up with that, too, so when you don't get your way now you can yell all you want, because we are still going to be heard.

So this is what we will do, we will make the hard choice. We know that the biggest concentration of liberals is in Hollywood, so we will hit them in their pocket books. This is a hard choice and we will start now. **1.) We will not attend any movies until we start to be heard, or at least until the 2010 elections.** The time until we are heard will be 2010 and maybe even get extended until 2012 the vote for the new president. Imagine if 40% of the public do not go to a movie until further notice. *Twilight* just made 750 million dollars for one weekend of one month that would be $300 million out of the pockets of liberals. Just imagine how it will hurt some pocket books. Instead we will go roller-skating, or Ice skating or get a pizza at a place like Chucky Cheese's, or a little raceway, or a bowling alley, or a riding stable, ECT. We will be creative, and we will have fun without the movies, the point is to not attend a movie, not on date night and especially on family night.

This should be easy for family night, after all how many movies are there that are not cartoons or animation that you can take your kids to and feel good about. Why does Hollywood make so many movies and so few "G" rated movies? Especially when the "G" rated movies make so much more money than the other ratings. There is a monetary motivator there as well and yet Hollywood doesn't make as many "G" movies. Why is that? They will make movies using gang members, rappers, vampires and glorify their life styles, or a dance movie where gang members are out in the streets dancing. As much as I would like to see that, I have to admit I have never seen any gangs dancing in the streets. Is Hollywood trying to corrupt or help cause chaos in our society by making these kinds of movies seem desirable? Why do they make these really stupid comedies and not making more "G" movies? It does seem to fit their pattern of trying to create chaos.

You have a director, Roman Polanski, who rapes a <u>teenage girl</u> and then he flea's the country. Later in his life he is apprehended, but because it happened years ago, he is no longer a child abuser. Thousands of other people are in prison for the abuse of children. The time limit on rape and murder does not expire, why should his crimes expire, because he is a celebrity. Now the reason I asked if Hollywood is trying to corrupt our society, is because even after knowing all of this, Hollywood actors and actresses come out to stand up for this child rapist.

Some really stupid comments came out about this subject. For example Whoopi Goldberg says, "It's not really rape-rape". What exactly does rape-rape mean? So is this what Hollywood is all about, no ethics. I wish we could get some conservatives together and start there own movie industry, like John Voigt and Chuck Norris. They can make G movies and the conservatives will flock to these movies. They could call it Holly world or something like that and start it somewhere near St. Louis the middle of the country instead of on the coast. They are creative, I am sure they could come up with something.

Back to the subject of this chapter; **1.) We will not attend any movies until we start to be heard.** If you don't think this will make a dent in redistribution of wealth, you are wrong. There are HUGE numbers of people who fall into the 40% of the American People who are conservatives. I consider Hollywood as the great bastion of liberalism. If all of us band together and do not attend movies that could be a huge number of dollars. For example if Hollywood yields $200,000.00 on a weekend and we take 40% of that away for that weekend, that is $80,000.00 a weekend. Now if we do that for an entire year we would take 4 billion 160 million dollars out of Hollywood liberals pockets. That stops $4,160,000,000.00 from getting into our liberal political candidates pockets for there campaigns. It will be much more than that if we do the same for the blockbuster movies. Let the liberals support their own industry, not us. This is pretty good for step 1 and this is only the beginning of our embargos. This is one of the difficult things we must do. We do not have to miss some of these movies because they will come out on DVD and we can watch them then. Hollywood will not crash without our support, but they will be hurt and that is the point. If we continue to get no respect and no mass media coverage, we band together, by not buying or renting there DVD's, which will also hurt their pocket books again. These things will make us feel like we are striking back, and not just sitting idly by and accepting this socialism, we will be doing something. It is better than being upset with this administration and doing nothing

Other things that should be important in our lives should be how our president treats other countries. President Obama did not attend the anniversary of the Berlin Wall coming down as if the wall coming down wasn't important enough of an event to attend. I do not understand why he values our association of our European allies so little. I speculate that it is the same reason that he pulled the missile radar units out of Europe. His agenda for Emperor of the World is more important than our European associations and our European Allies. His association with communist / socialist countries like Venezuela, Cuba, China and Muslim countries takes priority over Europe. Maybe he just did not attend the celebration of the wall coming down because the Earth Wind and Fire was performing in the White House again.

The president did not call the attack at Ft. Hood, on unarmed soldiers a Jihadist Terrorist attack. The President said no religion would condone this attack, but if it was a Muslim Jihadist who was behind the attack, he would have only killed the infidel dog because the Koran tells him so. If I understand the Koran correctly this kind of behavior would have been considered as favorably behavior.

Getting back to the embargoes, I can not emphasize this embargo enough; let's feel like we are doing something right now. We need to stop attending movies; again this is only the first step. If you want all of the steps to start doing them now, they are in appendix A in the back of the book. This will tell you all the ways we can fight back now and get started. By the word we, I mean the extremely poor to the rich <u>CONSERVATIVE PEOPLE</u> of our nation. These things can make huge differences if we band together.

We are not any different from our liberal counter part in the fact that we want our kids to do better in their life than we did in our life. The difference is that the liberals don't see how this communist/socialist agenda hurts our children's possibilities, because they believe that capitalism is bad, and that capitalism decreases our children's opportunities. When in reality it is capitalism that gives our children the best chance of having a better life then our own life. Why do people from so many countries want to move hear.

In each chapter, I will write about something that is dear to my heart. To start out I would like to take some time to write about the Stimulus Package. In this <u>Pork Package, not stimulus package,</u> this administration has actually created a slush fund for this administration to use at its leisure. I believe this administration is now trying to add to their slush fund by passing the health care bill, with it not taking effect until 2013, but yet the people will be taxed for it in 2011 which means these taxes will go into their slush fund. If reelected in 2010 and 2012 we may not be able to stop anything this administration has already set into motion so it is vital that we vote this administration out of office. On many occasions Hannity has talked about this slush fund on his television show and I believe him to be correct. For example, "spending millions of stimulus dollars about how something smells," this is not only stupid but not something that can stimulate the economy to create jobs. Another portion of the stimulus package is about fixing an airport that has a very low volume of air traffic, and thereby a useless a spending spree. This kind of thing goes on, and on in this stimulus package. Does it create jobs? Yes, the problem is that it creates small amounts of jobs and it will not employ anyone in many cases for even a year. In my home state of Minnesota I happen to know that some stimulus money went toward a bridge. Now I know that this bridge would have used federal funds sometime anyway. So why not build it now? The problem is it employed 34 people and I believe the bridge is already finished! Next there were 5 Minneapolis police salaries funded with stimulus money, but in three years Minneapolis will have to start paying their salaries, this only postpones the money and the state will have to pay. Now it turned out that since the economy in my state is so bad that they have laid off some police officers anyway.

This is a good thought, but again this is a temporary fix. The long term fix is nowhere to be seen. I have ill feelings towards our government simply because they are acting stupidly, and I say this because the government is not curing the problem. Creating 39 jobs for my state, 5 of them last 3 years and the other 34 lasted 6 months; this does not help my state's economy when our state lost over 100,000 jobs just since last year, only 99,966 jobs to go. Where's the relief? One of the things that would stimulate manufacturing would be tax breaks to set-up factories; this helps because the people with money and an idea as to how to start a business would get start-up tax breaks. The biggest cost in starting a business is the labor costs, those costs will always be there and will not change. The next thing in business, are the start-up costs. If people who were thinking about starting a factory and had a tax break there first year, they would be more likely start a factory. New business prospectors and venture capitalists are afraid to start businesses because of 2 major reasons; one this administration is not very open about how taxes are going to be charged, and the direction of federal policies; two, business owners are afraid of where this medical bill is going and how this administration will pay for it. If they get a public option, how much will the private businesses get charged for this medical bill? Let's say I was going to start a factory to make end tables, I want to know that if I invest my $500,000.00, that in the first year it would not be lost. This would be security in knowing I would not lose my $500,000.00 by having to declare Bankruptcy. The government is not going to bail out my little business, and there is no confidence in this administration for these kinds of businesses decisions.

On top of these concerns, let's say the government was going to give me start up tax breaks, and this medical insurance problem was fixed. I start my business, with 100 people in my factory, and 100 other people in my state do the same thing, then you have 10,000 people working in my state not to mention the 3-5 salesmen that will be hired, not to mention the trucks that will be hauling the materials to the factory and the trucks used to get the product to the retail stores. Finally imagine that this happens in all 50 states, you have just created a ½ a million jobs. The scary thing is that this simple concept isn't even in Washington. Maybe it is true that our President is a socialist and does want to keep people down. By this I mean jobless and dependent on a socialist government that hands you everything, food & money. With a Health care bill that pays for your health care. Unfortunately as president you get blamed for everything that goes wrong as well as getting credit for everything that goes right. Maybe president Obama is just trying to keep the people down until 2011 just before the next election and then he will pass some conservative ideas and start to bring back the economy and then blame the past depression/recession on Bush and the republicans, to try to get reelected.

I want to tell you about the Delta smelt. In California there is a 3" minnow in the smelt family that was put on the endangered species list and therefore it had to be saved. Now Governor Schwartzenegger and President Obama with all of there resources are not smart enough to figure out how stop these smelt from being killed in the pump at the damn that irrigates a ½ million acres and 100's of people in California are unemployed. This smelt also stops crop production. This kills capitalism, it stops the farmers from hiring workers, and it stops us from having more US crops. Maybe the President is trying to keep the people down, or in this case maybe we will just have to get China send us some of there crops since we are borrowing so much money from them every chance we get. So I am asking you to do another Embargo, **13. So what we need to do is to buy no Chinese products, no fruits and vegetables, no clothes, no games, no parts no anything.** All of these problems increase our human pain, because the Governor of California and this administration can't figure out a way to stop the smelt from getting into the pump or relocating these minnows for their survival. When an animal takes precedence over human development and the state employment and our economy is in a recession like in California and in a recession in the rest of the nation we still worry more about a minnow! Mr. President, do you want to talk about acting stupidly!

Where are our human values, why does a minnow come before our country? California wake up, with all of the entertainers in Hollywood why don't you create a concert, a tour across American and raise money for the state of California. You entertainers do it for aides, you will do it for stray or injured animals, even polar bears, and you will do it at the drop of the hat. Now when it appears your taxes are going higher every year you want to cry about it. Why don't you put together a tour and give the proceeds to the state and help California get back on track. Your Governor and your state needs your help, where is your patriotism. These are simple fixes and not permanent but a band aid sure feels good when you first get cut.

When our forefathers wrote the Declaration of Independence and then the constitution of the United States of America, they did this to unite a nation, and let everyone know that everyone was equal under God. These ideas were built upon Christian beliefs with room to accept any culture, religion, race, as long as they did not interfere with the privacy and moral rights of other human beings. They wanted to manage their own lives and tax their own lives, for the purpose of freedom from persecution, mostly for the freedom of persecution of their religious beliefs. You could get into this in depth and argue many of the intrinsic points, but basically you would have to agree with me that we had a revolution for our freedoms.

So my point is that this nation was founded under God. That was why the Pledge of Allegiance was written. *I pledge allegiance to the flag of the United States of America and to the Republic for which it stands, one Nation under God, indivisible, with Liberty and Justice for all.* Now some nut somewhere decides that they should not have to say the pledge allegiance in public schools because it says under God in it. So because of this nut we no longer say the pledge of allegiance in our schools, before starting school. When we take back our country we need to require the pledge of allegiance to be said in every elementary school in our nation. If they are not willing to say the pledge of allegiance we take their entire federal aide away and fine them. If someone feels so strongly that they are not willing to say the pledge allegiance they may just stand there quietly.

Why does a small group of people get to set policy on the rest of us, because they don't believe in god, why do they get to dictate policy? This is our country and we are taking it back. To make it fair there can even be a box on the presidential ballot that simply asks do you want your children to say The Pledge of Allegiance in school YES ___ NO___! And if we have a 60% majority we put the Pledge Allegiance back in the classroom. This is the type of political correctness that this country needs now!

SUMMARY

In chapter II I start to list embargos that we can use to fight liberalism. Again, embargos are the main point of this book. I will suggest more embargos as my book continues. If you think that I make sense with these embargos and this is the right thing to do, we will be uniting against this liberal social agenda.

Chapter III

Give me Liberty or Give me Sports

Rush Limbaugh was not allowed to buy a pro football team with a group of investors that made a bid for the St Louis Rams. Why was he denied from being a partner, within a group of buyers, for a pro football team? Some liberals made up some stuff about him, to make it look like he was prejudiced against black people; then some more liberals, Rev. Jessie Jackson and the Rev. Sharpton spoke out against him. He was forced to resign from the group or the group's odds to win this bid would go down. How come some liberals that claim to be reverends and can put their 2 cents in the sports industry as if what they have to say is important? Why is it when 1.8 million conservative Americans march on Washington, there is no mass media coverage? No one seems to care what we conservatives want to say. Yet any liberal can speak out against anything and the mass media covers it.

Back to the reason that Rush Limbaugh was run out of the sports industry was because they said he was prejudiced, and that black players wouldn't play for him, this is ridiculous. Even if he was prejudice, and I never heard him say anything that would indicate that he was prejudice. I also doubt if anyone would leave there multimillion dollar jobs because their boss is prejudice. If you pay me Millions of dollars and my new boss is prejudice against me because I am white and he is still willing to pay me millions of dollars, I don't care if he is prejudice. I will work for him and laugh all the way to the bank. They said that the teams are composed of 60% black players, and that is why it matters. Every audience I have ever been in at a game is at least 90% white, but that doesn't seem to matter, I do not think the players care if their taking white people's money or black people's money. The same as if they took money from Rush Limbaugh or someone else.

Now in fairness to that statement I have only attended games in the northern areas so I don't know if southern audiences or east or west coast audiences are predominantly white. If that is true around the rest of the country then it is white people who pay these black players their salaries. I really don't think black players; care whether their money comes from black people or white people. As a white person I know my ticket pays their salaries and I don't mind one bit even though a lot of these players have arrogant attitudes. How many times have you heard somebody say these athletes make way to much money? This is a conservative attitude in a liberal industry. It must be a liberal industry because of the amounts of money that the players, owners, coaches and people in this industry make. This must be a liberal industry if two liberal reverends can influence an industry that is not a religious industry. That is how two liberal men can make statements that influence the NFL owners to shun Rush Limbaugh? It is time to let these liberal sports franchise owners know that we have some power, a voice in this, because we pay the owners and players salaries with our tickets.

So another way we can make the government really take notice of us, the conservatives, is to attend no sporting events, within the first two weeks of every month. Do you think the Sports announcers will notice if the attendance is down 40% or more? Do you think our voices will be heard by not being there or by the owners not getting our money? I believe that we the conservatives are more than 40% of the fan base because conservatives try to keep a balanced budget in our household incomes and only after our household budgets are balanced do we buy our game tickets, we sometimes even budget all year long to buy our season tickets. We can use the president's redistribution of wealth agenda against his liberal followers in this embargo technique, which is another way of voting without waiting to vote. I am guessing, but from the leagues reaction to what 2 reverends say about Rush Limbaugh these owners are probably liberals, too. So we are hurting liberals in their pocket book again and making our voices be heard by empty seats at a professional sports event.

So back to what we can do now, voting without waiting to vote, another embargo on Liberal territories. **2. Attend** no Sporting events **in the 1ˢᵗ two weeks of every month.** This is another tough decision. Can you handle it? Is it more important to see a sporting event or more important to get our capitalistic economy back? After these communist/ socialist agendas get passed will any of us middle class people be able to afford to attend any sporting events and none of the lower class will ever be able to go to a professional sporting event. If you have already paid for season tickets, and you watch the game at home, your empty seat does not support the local parking, restaurants and venders at the game, and your empty seat is being heard. You are making a statement by your empty seat. You already know when enough seats are not purchased the game maybe blacked out, which means you may even have to listen to the game on the radio. Are you really prepared to do that? That is what these embargos are all about. We the people, have a voice and can make a dent in the liberal's pocket books if we stick together then we will be heard. If we can get Conservative Corporations to join us and not buy empty seats during the first 2 weeks of every month, it is another show of power. Many businesses are afraid to make business decisions because of this administration. Still after a year in office this new administration is not clear about taxes and policies. So many major businesses are still anxious about making business decisions. Hopefully they will join us in our non-attendance to not be seen.

Back to the problem at hand, if we don't go to sporting events what will we do. We can go to Semi pro games, arena football, college sports or even high school sporting events. And not just football games, we will do the same with hockey, basketball, baseball, tennis, golf and all professional sports. This is what we did when the football strike went on a few years back, and what we did when baseball went on strike for almost the entire season, we can go on without sports if we have to. What I am suggesting is another embargo that we the people with a conservative attitudes can do to make the major sports teams take notice, that again we the people (conservatives) can make a big difference in the attendance at the games. This will be our voice, by not being there; Washington will take notice of what we are doing, because we are not at the game the mass media will notice. Another hard decision, can you make this decision as well. These are my suggestions so far and I will have a hard time following them as well, but if we band together they will have to hear our voice. Believe it or not this is the most important embargo, because our absence will really make a statement. If you decide not to do this one you are not really worried about this country. Please read my embargos and talk to people about these embargos and adhere to them, please. If we start this and it does not seem to take effect stick with it more and more people will join us as time goes on.

I love football and I like going to movies so these embargos hurt me as well. I stated earlier that I live in Minnesota and this year the Vikings have may be a real contender, but I will follow my own embargos, will you? This administration has already called the, Tea Party Members Nazi's when the Democrats are the ones with the communist agenda's, and that we are their enemy. They say that we are a violent group, when the only beatings have come from the unions controlled by the Democrats. Why is that mister president? If you can't have your way you send in the unions to strong arm people at town hall meetings with the Chicago style of politics. If you think something is good for the public, you force it on them. Almost needless to say, I don't like your agendas, I am a not a Nazi but I am going to stand up for my God given unalienable right?

I don't like or want your communist/socialist agendas. This empting of the seat at professional sports events will be noticed by the mass media, but it is one of the hardest decisions you will make, especially if you have to listen to your team on the radio. We have to band together on this embargo more than all of the other embargos that I am suggesting because it will get mass media coverage.

I told you I want to bring up a subject that needs to be written about in every chapter. Almost every person I have ever talked to agrees with me that these professional athletes make way to much money. Most of them make more money in one season than I will probably make in my entire life time. When they have a wining season the owners threaten to leave the city if we don't give them a new stadium. Then the franchise holds the city hostage by way of a city tax referendum. When the owner made most of his money off of his present fan base, where is his loyalty? All of this is done in the disguise of capitalism. If I can make more money somewhere else why should I stay here? Remember where your roots are. If you want to be respected for something other than being a great Athlete, be a humanitarian. Players could pool some of their big paychecks and give back to the community by not passing out free turkeys but by combining your money and build something the community can really use, like low income housing and donate it to the community with a name on it like VIKING PARK! A few years back I heard about a player that gave out a house every year to someone in the community. This is true humanitarianism.

The arrogance of some of these big name players is just unreal. They seem to forget where they came from and where their roots are. Instead of giving something back to the community where they play or even where they grew up, they save many of their millions for their children, I respect that, but they make enough that they can do both and give something back to the communities where they work or grew up.

I called this chapter give me liberty or give me sports and I was not kidding because you have to be willing to give up sports. There are only 3 justifying reasons that I can give you for this embargo, the obvious one is that the empty seats will have the mass media notice us, we will hurt the liberals pocket books, and empting seats especially on winning teams would show some of these arrogant players that we pay their check. Those are the 3 reasons. I have been a resident of Minnesota my whole life so I grew up with the Vikings, I love to see them winning but now if we have to pay for their new stadium, I may have to say good bye to the Vikings. I just do not believe we should have to pay for their stadium.

I believe that this is an issue of capitalism and that with all of the money and support that we the fans give the Vikings, they should finance their own stadium by at least 75%. If they are not willing to put up their share they can move to another city that will build them a stadium. I do not want to see them go, but one ticket not to mention tickets for a family of 6 costs me a lot of money. I just do not want a referendum tax on top of ticket costs. I heard the cheap play off tickets were $600.00, that is $3,600.00 for my family

We have another embargo that hit them directly where it hurts. The media refuses to cover us. There is no good way to do it, but the only way we can really hurt them is this. If you are a conservative and you do not believe that this Media covered the conservative's side of any of these issues, then we will have to put a stop to this. The wall street journal is the one news paper that many Americans get for financial news. Keep this subscription. Cancel every other Subscription. If you need something for business then start a subscription with the Wall Street Journal. If the Wall Street Journal wants to survive they had better start covering the issues that are of interest to the conservatives as well as the liberals of this country. If they can not start to cover both sides of an issue we will cancel that subscription as well. Do I want these newspapers companies to go out of business? Yes I do. The reason is very simple, because they show the Democratic/ Liberal side to every story and do not give you a view of the Republican/Conservative side on any issues. Newspapers were supposed to be the watch dog for the people telling everything about what is going on in our nation. It is not their job to decide what is right or wrong!!! Just tell us, the American people what is going on.

If we do this, cancel our subscriptions to some papers and some magazines, some may go under. Yes they will have to declare bankruptcy, I understand that they will have to lay some people off and create some unemployment. If a local paper covered the Tea party events keep your subscription, but if they did not cover the tea party events cancel your subscription. I know this unemployment is a bad thing right now, but they should have covered both sides; it is their job. Of all the major stories, they should have covered the Tea Parties, and they did not. If you feel you need read about what is going on in this country, you can call fox news to order Newsmax a fox networks magazine.

When I was a kid the news media would have been all over this A.C.O.R.N. issue. With them accepting money from the government, then giving money to the Democratic Party, by supporting President Obama is wrong. I don't care if the money goes to a different fund if it is within the same company! No Company should be able to take federal, state or local government money and then give campaign contributions to the Democratic or Republican Party. Then there were some issues about a year ago with ballot tampering. How come there aren't newsmen all over that. That just smells like a conspiracy, and they are not even interested. So this is what I am going to ask you to do. This will be the third Embargo that we will be placing on the Liberals.

3.) We are going to cancel all subscriptions to magazines and newspapers, except the wall street journal if we need it for work, and subscribe with the wall street journal, again, only if we need it for work. If the wall street journal does not show the conservative side of the story by June of 2010 we will cancel that subscription as well. We need to have some control or some power over our own lives. Unfortunately the Mass Media from television can not be hit this manner.

Now the Mass media does not cover the story about how leaks for this global warming has got out, which should be a huge story. Yet no one is covering it. This Mass Media's double standard coverage is so bad it is obvious. John Kerry's daughter got a DUI ticket in California no mass media coverage. If that was Sarah Palin's daughter with a DUI, the mass media would have been all over it. This double standard is what the newspapers must also pay for.

For many years negative things that happened to the Republican Party and they were reported but not when the negative things happened to the Democratic Party it was not reported or reported late and without any vigor. Would you be surprised to learn that on several occasions the Clinton Administration conducted bombings? Bombings that had minor coverage in the news, yet they happened. The news media made decisions that apparently they thought were essential for the security of this country. However no military decisions by the Bush Administration were ever considered essential for the security of the country, another double standard. The newspaper or television leadership has no right to make those decisions for the American people. So now we the conservatives can make at least the newspaper portion of the mass media pay for these decisions. I am not sorry for this embargo, because I also believe that these kinds of decisions are why their businesses are in danger of failing today. They should have covered both sides of these issues for years.

Now once again the national news media does not cover much about how the Climate change groups have falsified documentation. The Mass Media does not even start to talk about that until 2 weeks later or more. Why is the Mass

Media waiting so long to ask the questions, is it because they are in bed with this Administration or are they just covering his back? That is correct they are giving them enough time to come up with some reasons to explain the global warming issues.

Again if we the conservatives are 40% of the American Public we can at least really hurt the newspapers and magazine industry that refuse to cover the conservative side of many issues, especially with the health care bill and the stimulus package accounts. Why is it that these Czars of President Obama's are being paid for with my taxes, the ethics committee should be looking into that and why are there so many of them? Why is no one looking at personal care attendants of Michelle Obama, estimated in excess of 20 persons. In comparison, I heard Farrah Fawcett only needed 5 and she was the most beautiful woman in that world in her day. Who is paying for the Earth Wind & Fire at the White House? I hope that is coming out of the Presidents personal funds, because I am a tax payer and his personal expense account needs to be cut off, if it is coming out of U.S. taxes. I find it hard to believe that the President hasn't heard that the country is in a recession. Where does he get off throwing my tax dollars around?

There is a rumor that President Obama never ordered the Navy Seal team to take out the pirates that saved the captain of the Meresk. Now this is a rumor, but it does seems to fit president Obama's inability to make a decision. I wonder if a junior officer on site, made a command decision that was relative to the situation, because that is what they are taught. In the military you are taught at a young age in your career to lead, to make a decision. As a military leader, there is nothing is worse than indecision. President Obama took 3-4 months to make a decision about troops needed to go into Afghanistan. Granted, it takes some time to consider all the options, but shouldn't it go faster with all those Czars his on staff?

SUMMARY

In Chapter III, I wrote about how Rush Limbaugh did not get a fair opportunity to buy a football team, because some liberals said some things about him to make it seem like he was prejudice. This is one of the liberal techniques that we are fighting.

I also wrote about the newspapers not giving the conservatives equal time on the other side of the argument, whatever the subject might be, and how that might be the reason they are in danger of going under. Again, I am just keeping this a simple how to book.

Chapter IV
Cash Ford Clunkers

Our president decided to give General Motors stimulus money. General Motors (GM) took this money from the government making GM the new Government Motors. When GM took this stimulus money maybe they didn't realize how much power the government would actually have. However; I don't believe that, GM's lawyers went through the government contract with a great deal of detail. Then after they accepted the contract, Barrack Obama as the president of the United States of America, fired the CEO of GM. Then a line of very small cheap cars came out. I wonder if these cheap cars are really safe. I am sure that the President's green agenda had a hand in this. Everyone knows that these green jobs only last a short time, so cash for clunkers was created to help support GM's and Chrysler corporation sell their cars. Unfortunately all of the automotive industry benefited from cash for clunkers and not just GM and Chrysler Corporation. In fact I heard that the foreign car industry benefited even more from this than did American car companies. In fact truly poor people couldn't even get in on cash for clunkers unless their clunker was already paid off. I have a clunker and I could not use this program because my clunker was not paid off. I am not poor I am middle class, but how many poor people have there car paid off? Most don't, so most could not even participate in this tax rebate.

I called this chapter Cash Ford Clunkers, because Ford Motor Company was the only major American car company that did not take stimulus money and they are still making profits. This was not a typo, but it was a play on words.

There are so many things wrong with this move by the president that it is scary.

- THE PRESIDENT SHOULD HAVE <u>NO CONTROL</u> IN ANY COMPANY IN THE PRIVATE SECTOR, while he is holding the office of president.
- I also think that most people believe that the government should not be bailing out the private sector.
- Any time money is given out it is tax money that means that it is <u>my money,</u> as well as every other American taxpayer; and I believe that congress takes this task of spending our tax money too lightly. As a tax payer I never would have approved the bailing out GM.
- Lastly the president should not be able to regulate the kinds of cars we drive, the most government should do in the private sector is to make recommendations, or safety requirements that would protect the public, and it should be proposed by congress our Representative's.

I don't know if you remember, but this is the second time that Chrysler has been bailed out. So are we seeing a trend from the auto industry, I think this is another reason most Americans think the Auto industry should sink or swim on their own merit. How many times will Chrysler and Gm need to be bailed out in the future and in the name of saving jobs? Every time there is a recession will they be standing there with their hand out, this is twice for Chrysler. The flip side of the Chrysler Corporation getting a second bail out is that the Ford Corporation made a Billion dollar profit in the 3rd quarter. Keep in mind that Chrysler and GM did not, when they both received government bail out money and also had the cash for clunkers program. The cash for clunkers was a government designed program to help the public to buy GM and Chrysler cars. Did this help stimulate their business? It did, but it seemed to help all of the other auto corporations as much maybe even more then GM and Chrysler.

What can we do to show this government that we do not approve of the way they are running our country? I actually think that the cash for clunkers was a good attempt to stimulate the economy; the problem is this administration is thinking about the short term success but not about the long term effect. So what are we going to do about it? We are going to do this, 4. **We will only buy Ford and Saturn cars, or just buy American based cars no foreign cars.** Another hard decision, so again can you handle the hard decision? I love my Cadillac, but it is the last GM or Chrysler I will ever buy. I just recently bought a ford focus. From now on the one good Car our family will have will be a Lincoln Town Car. The other family cars we will have will be the ford focus unless I can get better gas mileage with a Saturn. Now again if you follow this embargo technique we will hurt the liberals in their pocket book again. We also tell the president some things.

The things we are telling the president is that we are not going to pay our hard earned tax money for a car and then turn around and pay for it again. If you are a GM or Chrysler employee and a conservative I understand why you do not feel comfortable following with this embargo. I also know that being employed by GM or Chrysler is a good paying job, so I do not expect you to follow this embargo, but you know as well as I do that if GM and Chrysler go bankrupt they will not be out of business for long. You will not be out of work long. If you are an employee and you see what is going on with this government, you need to make a commitment to your nation. If you don't want your pay to be regulated by the pay Czar since you're owned by the government now, you have to get rid of this administration. After the president fired your CEO, what would make you think he can't fire you? This Administration is trying to get this Health Care bill past and then they will be able to fire you if you are a smoker or you have diabetes, or something else stupid. You do not want this government control, isn't the union control enough for you to deal with.

The Government is planning another stimulus package supposedly to help small businesses and with more shovel ready projects that did not work in the first stimulus and it will not stimulate the Economy. I am not for another stimulus package because this administration doesn't address the true problems, <u>for example jobs.</u> The things planned in the stimulus package do not really stimulate the economy in fact the Cash for Clunkers was the only thing that really helped the economy and it really was a tax rebate. In the auto industry the bottom will fall out if you keep giving a rebate to everybody that buys a car, because people will wait for the next rebate before they buy their next car. In other words after everyone has a car using this program no one will buy their next new car for 6 months to a year.

Another reason that we need to buy ford cars is because of the president's redistribution of wealth agenda. The president takes over GM and Chrysler, and then we see the redistribution of wealth come into play. We can counter this. Think about it. If we the conservatives; rich to poor; just buy our cars at Ford or Saturn dealerships we can ignore the presidents redistribution of wealth agenda and vote without waiting to vote, again with another embargo. We will be putting our money into American Capitalism. We will also have a secure stock to buy and invest in. We the Conservatives 40% of Americans are buying Ford and Saturn vehicles these two companies will become solid companies. So the 40% of us conservatives have to stop buying Volvo's, Mercedes, and GM's Chryslers Volkswagens and so on. At least until we are heard. So this is what we are going to do, **5. When we buy our next car, van or truck we buy Ford's and Saturn's.**

Many of us are really pissed at these agenda's, regarding the redistribution of wealth. This administration thinks there is nothing we can do until the elections in 2010 and 2012. They practically own the mass media so they can have things they want blocked from getting televised, and they believe they can block our voices in the same manner, so these embargos will put a stop to this, so I am proposing ways to fight back without creating a revolution. The last thing I want is to be credited for is any kind of act of violence. This is the reason that I came up with the embargo idea. The liberals would not even have us conservatives planning this and then employing these embargos, if the news media would have just covered our Tea Parties to begin with. Blame the mass media. So for silencing us, we will fight back with these embargos. The thought of "I heard a nut yelling at my TV and realized that nut was me," is becoming more common.

Again, I relate back to the woman crying to Rush on the radio. She asked Rush several times what are we going to do about the current situation. The only answer that she got from Rush was to continue to call her congressmen. The congressmen are starting to shut off there phones, and believing that they are right and that we are idiots so they are still trying to pass these bills and without even listening to their constituents. The thing that we can do to fight that is to vote these liberals out of office in 2010 and 2012. This turning off your phones is not something we have to put up with. There are other ways of being heard. We need to continue to call our Representatives and Congressman in Washington and at their office in their home state.

There was an increase in the 3rd Quarter of 2009; why; because of cash for clunkers, a tax break actually created some very minor economic stimulus. Yes we need more tax breaks like these. Unfortunately this administration is not very good at original ideas and they can't even run the cash for clunkers forever. They did not even run cash for clunkers very good when you consider all they had to do was write out checks against the cars that were traded in. How are these Harvard grads going to run something as massive as a country of 300 plus million people's health care system? These people in this administration are Theorists. What that means to us is that they have no business experience or very little experience only ideas that they hope will work. What they are putting into practice are things they believe to be good, but have never actually put into practice. Just from what they have done so far their theories are not working. I thought as Harvard Grads; that after their theories that they put into practice that did not work; their empirical evidence would tell them to use traditional techniques. They might be doing this with their second stimulus via small businesses. If they are not careful they will really hurt small businesses, because small businesses do not have unlimited resources and capital to adjust their businesses.

Look at this stimulus package that these theorists passed because our country was in a crisis, the only part of their stimulus package that actually created a small stimulus in our economy was their cash for clunkers program and that only cost a few billion dollars which was actually a tax rebate. Look at the green jobs, in reality they only last a very short time. Now you might think that I am against the green movement, but I am not, as long as it actually pays in the long term and helps us save energy. Let's be clear right here, this industry does not create long term jobs. Look at the TARP money; that was loaned to banks with the idea of strengthening the financial community, this money was to be used for loans. That Tarp money was meant to stimulate loans, but the government wants banks to risk this money on high risk loans that may not be paid back and the banks are not willing to do that. Now supposedly there has been $200 billion paid back, which is the way it was designed and now the president wants to put it back into his slush fund, I mean to stimulate small businesses. He seems to be using this slush fund to convince congressmen to vote a certain way with millions given to there state.

If you do not believe that our senators are being coerced with money for their districts; look at Senator Landruie from Louisiana who received $300 million dollars to vote, to allow the medical bill to go in front of congress to be debated. Where is your ethics senator? Is there anything you wouldn't do for money? Now everyone knows you can be bought. You may think that you did it for your constituents, but your ethics are now in question by your constituents. You should definitely blame Senator Landrieu whether this bill passes congress or not. If she would not have sold her vote it would not even have gone in front of congress.

The Biggest issue here is financial responsibility. This Administration is constantly talking about financial responsibility. They have $200 billion and they want to use it to help small businesses which should create jobs, yet nothing this administration has done has created any jobs. That's right, they are planning on using it to create jobs by way of the small businesses; I wonder if ACORN is considered a small business. This Administration should be starting to pay off this massive deficit that they have created. If we the individual home owners were given $200,000.00 we would pay off our home if we could, we would not go out and buy another house. Then we would use the house payment money to pay off our bills until we were debt free, we would be so relieved, but yet this administration wants to spend this money on things similar to what they have already done and has already been proved not to work.

Take the medical healthcare bill that is so stupid that some seniors think there health care is being taken away. Seniors will be charged more for their medical care if this bill passes. Not only are they being charged more, but we (the taxpayers) will be getting charged for it as well. God help us, because I have little faith in this administration and the way this Administration is running our country.

I do not believe that the Conservative American people think that taking $200 Billion Dollars and allowing this Administration to put it into small businesses will cure America's job problems.

SUMMARY

In chapter IV, I also talked about how the President bought the power to fire the CEO of GM. How the President got a line of small cheap cars to be produced. This is one of the reasons we the people who understand conservatism can not let the president take over private businesses, fire CEO's and get away with it. We at least need to try to stop this.

I also mentioned how and why we should buy Ford and Saturn stock as an investment. I also started to write about how this stimulus package did not stimulate our economy, and we need jobs. These are the important things that this Administration seems to be missing in their attempts. This is another reason why this how to book with these embargos got started.

Chapter V
In Bed with Big Oil Companies

The democrats are always saying that we the Republicans are in bed with the big oil companies. We were getting our gas for under $2.00 per gallon and now it is $2.50 per gallon, you might believe that these actions are coming from the oil companies, but a great deal of that increase is from the taxes that the Democratic Party has put on your gas. The Democrats have also taxed your liquor and cigarettes. Didn't the President promise that he would not raise your taxes, just wait until cap and trade passes if the Democrats can get that to pass congress! Think about how this is hurting the American people during a recession. The democrats just love saying that republicans are in bed with the big oil companies. In fact there is a commercial here in Minnesota that has Michelle Bachman with oil on her and everyone she touches gets oil on them. This is so stupid, because of all the big companies that the Democrats are in bed with. So let's take a look at all the big corporations that the Democrats are in bed with.

Let's start with the banking system-Troubled Asset Relief Program (T.A.R.P.) money, give all that money to the banks in the disguise of strengthening the banks, so the Democrats are in bed with the banks.

Then the SEIU union show up at the town halls, do the Democrats own them, because they have started to show up at all of the town halls across America. Why was that, because of all of the violence we the Tea Party People have caused? Oh wait there wasn't any violence until the SEIU union actually showed up and then they beat someone up and this situation is finally going through the court system and these SEIU members are the ones that are on trial. So the Democrats are in bed with the Unions.

Let's not forget A.C.O.R.N. another Democrat organization that gave Obama's Campaign Fund, some money and now A.C.O.R.N. gets federal funding, that has to be illegal. Not to mention the voting fraud accusations, and the accusations that they tried to help set-up brothels. After all of these accusations the Democrats are still in bed with ACORN.

Then another big business that the democrats are in bed with is A.I.G. and this administration saved A.I.G. with stimulus money and saved their jobs, not created jobs. At least that was the reason this administration gave them money. It appears that this Administration was trying to control A.I.G. the same way they took over GM, but could not quit take over. So the Democrats are in bed with A.I.G.

Then there was the auto workers, another big union that the president wants to control, and now the Auto Workers Union have that "I saved your jobs" hanging over their heads. If you are one of those auto workers who was out of work for a while, Obama did not save your job. Yes some of you were out of work at one point or another, but do you really believe if the president would not have delegated stimulus money to GM and Chrysler that they really would have folded. Even if they would have declared bankruptcy, I don't think that they would have ever folded. More proof that the Democrats are in bed with another Union.

The Democrats are in bed with the Chinese, on these loans, maybe with the water not hitting the fields in California so we have to buy Chinese vegetables. Think about that California, you are in a recession and the President, and your Governor seem to be more interested in doing the bidding of the Chinese then being interested in saving these farms and farming jobs in your state. You really need a Republican Governor who is a conservative because Arnold Schwarzenegger is a liberal governor in republican clothes. You need to find a conservative to replace him.

What about being in bed with the Global Warming movement, they had to change their name to Climate Change, because the weather was not helping there movement. Now it has been proved to be a hoax, so they kicked a couple of their scientists out of the climate change movement. They got caught with this fraudulent data and they the climate change people are still pushing for this carbon footprint tax. That is right they used fraudulent data to prove there point and then when there're proved a fraud, they kick those scientists out of their Climate Control movement and the president is still pushing this climate control agenda. I know why they are not changing this push because the New World Order needs this climate change stuff in order to charge you a for a carbon footprint. The Climate Change people are not letting this hacker that broke into their E-mails and proved these lies; to stop them from pushing for this carbon footprint tax. But if there is no real climate change problem then there is no carbon footprint tax. So Obama can not reach his goal of Emperor of the world without the carbon footprint tax.

The real problem is that if you lie about the time of day that the temperature is recorded by as little even by 10 minutes, you are adjusting your records. Adjusting your data is a lie, and the fact is that any time you adjust data, you are lying. Any time you lie when you are in an organization, that organization loses their reputation and becomes a non-reputable source. So nothing that Angola University has done should be acceptable in the scientific community.

One of our local weathermen has never ever believed in this Global Warming stuff, because his data has had Minnesota as cooling. So again the Democrats are in bed with Global Warming.

They are in bed with the American Medical Association (AMA) when the AMA only has about 17% of the general practitioners belonging to it but the President needs the AMA's support to help them pass their medical health care bill and to push our country closer to socialism to help the president in his run for Emperor of the world.

They're in bed with the drug companies, because after Obama's secret meeting with the Pharmaceutical companies, the pharmaceutical companies start to run adds for his Public-Option Health Care bill. Why would they do this unless they believed that they would be getting something out of this?

Their in bed with AARP because AARP is going along with this Public Option Health Care bill because AARP has been told that they will be the only ones using a gap insurance and they will make a pretty penny. Why AARP does not see that some day they will be shut out is beyond me. If this administration who is trying to take over 1/6 of our economy will one day say how hard could it be to take over the gap insurance and then AARP will left with nothing.

They must be in bed with the Mass Media Television and Newspapers otherwise you would see many investigations like in the banks, SEIU A.C.O.R.N., the loans from the Chinese, this stimulus package-that appears to be a pork package, the pharmaceutical company's closed door meeting, the AARP closed door meeting, and the brawl beatings that the Democratic representatives took behind closed doors to get the public option to pass in the house 218 to 215. We are wondering since the door was closed were these representatives given stimulus package money or campaign contributions via ACORN. Since the doors were closed on many of these meetings we will never know the truth, and because the doors were closed we can believe anything that we want. That is the way this Administration conducts its transparent policies, by closing the doors.

After the Democrats being in bed with; the banking system, SEIU, A.C.O.R.N., A.I.G., the Auto Workers Union, GM and Chrysler, the Chinese, the global warming group, A.A.R.P., the pharmaceutical companies, the A.M.A., and let's not forget the mass media; you would think that they would not be pointing any fingers, but yet they do point their finger at the republicans for being in bed with the oil companies. Count them there are 12 different big businesses that the Democrats are in bed with. These are only the obvious ones; some of not so obvious are the Unions in general, we haven't even mentioned the gay community who is already upset with this Administration, probably the actor's guild and the writers union. The liberals in the Sports industry are probably in bed with this Administration as well. This list probably goes on and on, and the problem with a list this long is that they are all there with their hands out.

If you listen to the stories that the president tells, not one of these stories are about white people unless they are about women, so if you are a white man forget about getting anything from this government. The only white males that would get any recognition from this White House are Military men, although, the CIA and the Navy seals seem to be getting the cold shoulder from this white house, too. So if you are a white male and you have no affiliation with the military this administration does not care about you. I really don't care about that, because of all of the years that the black people were second class citizens, even after the Declaration of Independence and after the Gettysburg Address the black people in America did not get true respect in fact even today most black people have to do better then white people at interviews to get jobs. The problem is that the President seems to have affiliated himself with black men that want to change America toward socialism, not the black men and women who have been successful in business or successful in the military. That would make more sense, then to be affiliated with well educated theorists. I got some stats from the Rush Limbaugh's radio show; that seems to be relative here.

- Reagan's Administration had 58% of experience Cabinet Members.
- Bush senior had 52% of experienced Cabinet Members.
- Clinton had 37% of experienced Cabinet Members.
- Bush had 55% of experienced Cabinet Members.
- Obama has 8% of experienced Cabinet Members.

Maybe it is just me but it would seem to make sense that you would surround yourself with successful men and women in their field of any minority rather then people that are theorists and have no substantial private sector successes.

In each chapter I want to touch on some things that bothered me, and in this chapter it is terrorism. The issue of the terrorists that were detained and are being tried in this country is extremely stupid for 4 reasons. The first reason is that these trials will be in New York State and will cost New York State taxes. The second reason is that you are telling people who lost loved ones in this terrorist attack, that these WAR CRIMINALS should have the same rights as our own U.S. Citizens. Third it is like rubbing salt in a wound; because these are the actual people that planned the killing and killed their loved ones. Fourth if they do not get a death sentence and these detainees go to our prisons, these terrorists will be able to teach prisoners the radical Jihadist ways.

A lot of prisons are gang members. Many gang members, joined gangs because were looking for family link, which they could not find at home. Many Prisoners also have a low intellect and some mild mental illness. Since many mental hospitals are closed, and they have to go somewhere to serve time for the crime they committed, so they go to prison. All of these kinds of people are prime candidates to be converted to the Muslim religion, but this radical Jihadist Muslim heritage is not the kind of prisoners we want being released from our prisons and on to our streets. They can start more cells, or they can be taught how to build bombs or link up with other cells. We do not want this kind of prisoner released. The kind of prisoners that are convinced to hate other US Citizens, bomb U.S. Citizens and just cause chaos upon their release.

This Administration does not think about the results of what they do. If this Administration would have thought ahead they would have talked to prison officials and they would have found out that radical Jihadist perspective is taught in the prisons. This Administration does not do their homework. If we have military tribunals for these terrorists all of these problems are cured. Federal taxes are used instead of New York State taxes and they can still have a private lawyer if they want. War criminals do not have the same rights as us citizens and the military recognizes them as war criminals. These men have terrorized our country with terrorist acts that have killed U.S. citizens. These terrorists should not have the rights of U.S. citizens, because they are not U.S. citizens. New York City would not have salt rubbed in their wounds and justice will still be served. These terrorists are more likely to get the death sentence in a military tribunal and if they don't receive the death penalty they will be placed in a military prison where they will be kept separate from other prisoners and this Jihadist radicalism will not spread, from these terrorists to American prisoners.

SUMMARY

In chapter V, I wrote about how the Democrats are always claiming that we the Republicans are in bed with Oil Companies and I showed how the Democrats are in bed with lots of Big Corporations, and the Democrats are still pointing the finger at the Republicans. It is remarkable how this Administration does not even care that you know how many corporations they are in bed with.

Chapter VI

Americans Against Retired People (AARP)

The reason I called this chapter Americans Against retired people is because AARP is only behind this medical bill because AARP has the correct kind of gap insurance: that most other companies don't have and would make a killing on while other insurance companies would go under. There are other insurance companies that have this same kind of insurance.

What is wrong with this Public Option Insurance? There are so many things wrong with this Bill it is unreal. The only people who are behind this bill are the people who see the real ramifications of this bill which is a communist/socialist way of life, or the people who are seeing this as another hand out from the government, or maybe the illegal aliens that will be covered by this bill, or those very few people who don't know how good our medical system really works.

So what we are going to do is this, like me **6. you need to cancel your AARP insurance because there are**

other companies that do the same thing now. Some of you may need to help some of your elderly parents. I also understand that your parents may not want to change, but AARP does not support their interests any more. Now let's get into what is wrong with this Government Medical Care Bill. The very first thing I am going to say about this is simple; WE HAVE THE BEST HEALTHCARE IN THE WORLD: the health care insurance costs are the real problem. There are ways to fix this rising costs of insurance without taking over the entire health care system. If you take over the entire health care system you will be putting 10,000's of people out of work, many of the people that work for private insurance companies are going to be put out of work, and again this administration will be adding to the unemployment rate. First I will write about how we can fix our present system, and that the Democrats don't want to fix our present system they just want the control over the Heath Care in our country, and they are going to ruin our health care system.

Do not worry if this bill is passed we really can fix that later, it will be extremely difficult but we can do it. To be fair to the Democrats, they have elected President Obama, and they have the belief that he will change our country in the way that they want. When Bush was elected I had a lot of the same views as he did, so I was not worried about the direction our country was moving. The main reason was that I new he was a religious man and I felt secure in that. Most Democrats do want our country to balance its budget and to reduce the deficit and have a strong national defense. Our differences are in the way the far left has changed things. The Democrats have that same belief in Obama, the difference is that the general public is not hearing the conservative side of the news because they listen to the mass media, and the mass media does not report these conservative concerns.

So now I am going to write about the differences, and hopefully how to overcome them. I sincerely believe that most Democrats don't know what is actually going on. From the simple things like, I understand that the president's wife has 20+ attendants. She can have 50 for all I care if her husband is paying for them and not my taxes. The president has 30+ Czars or so again he can have 50 if he is paying for them and not my taxes. I understand Earth, Wing, and Fire play regularly at the White House, and again that is fine if President Obama is paying for that and he is not using my taxes. My point is I don't believe the Democrats as well as most of the American public are aware of this kind of Government waste.

Now I want to get into this Health Care Bill and explain some things about this bill that my Democratic friends at work did not know about this bill. The Democrats simply believe that it is for the poor who can't afford Health Insurance, and for preexisting conditions. If that would be the case no one would be against it, but eventually everyone will be on it, and extreme cost is what the conservatives don't like.

First I want to tell you about what the republicans have tried to get in these bills. Although this was supposedly a bi-partisan bill, these concepts were excluded, and not even considered. This bill may change by the time this book comes out, but that is not a big problem because the concepts that the republicans want in this bill, will not be in there, because up to this point none of these concepts have been in any of these proposed bills, and the Democrats bills for the most part have remained relatively the same.

- If this Healthcare bill is passed there will be no Health savings plans. When you think about the hospital costs being so high a health savings plans could reduce a hospital bill immensely, especially if you have had your health savings account for years, it could save your family from a bankruptcy. This bill will get rid of Health savings plans.

- If we created competition across state lines this would reduce health insurance costs, we do this simply by allowing insurance companies to compete nation wide instead of state wide. This is real competition. Not the kind of competition that you have by having the government run it because eventually it will force the private sector out of business because they can not compete with the unlimited funds of the government, causing more unemployment.

- Reforming the Lawsuit criteria in the same manner the auto industry has reformed it. That is called tort reform and the main concept that the Republicans want but it is nowhere in any of these bills proposed by the Democrats. The auto insurance companies reformed their lawsuit industry and they are still in business. I heard this item by itself could save $54 billion dollars a year, and yet tort reform is not in this bill. Most Democrats agree with this point, they just don't realize that it is not in this bill. Many Lawyers make a lot of the lawsuit money that they get for you. They could get as much as 60% in lawyer fees from your hardship.

- Why can't we allow doctors to see patients without insurance and allow the doctors to write it off on their taxes, this would allow every citizen in the United States of America to be covered and then we would not have to worry about existing conditions or if you are between jobs and if someone has no coverage? This was a concept I heard Glen Beck suggest and I think this is a great Idea. In my personal experience, my sister was taken ill with brain cancer while insured and living in Chicago. We brought her home with us to Minnesota, because she could no longer care for herself. We could not use her insurance because she wasn't working any longer and we crossed state lines. We got her Cobra, insurance which is very expensive and designed for those people without insurance; at least it is in the state of Minnesota. What wasn't covered by cobra was covered by the clinics donations. My wife works at the hospital associated with this clinic and she gives money to this clinic out of every pay check. Most of the employees give to this clinic. Most clinics have some kind of contributors. Do you think if the government takes over the health care system, people will continue giving donations to this clinic, NO, because the government can pay for it. We the people help support these kinds of charities everywhere because it is the right thing to do. This country really does help itself. So let's not rebuild the best health care system in the world and let's not have the government take over our Medical Care.

- Another thing that would help our health care system is deferred tax credits for things like wheel chairs and crutches or even as much as an operation for these people that are uninsured or have an existing condition and are between jobs. These kind of ideas would again be less expensive then any 2.5 trillion dollar health care bill, which is really just a grab for power by this Democratic Liberal Administration.

• Another thing that we could do is to extend health insurance benefits from the company you just left, if we pay for them after we leave. Maybe we could create a national fund from all employed people everywhere in this country. This could be funded with $1.00 a week from every employee. This fund could be used to pay these extended health care benefits. This is alone the lines of a concept I heard on the Rush Limbaugh talk show.

These are the things that the Republican Party have had in different bills and they have tried to get them passed, because they believe these things will really fix the health care insurance problems, especially the tort reform because that would reduce insurance premiums immensely. We the Republicans are called the party of no by the Democrats because we say no to the Democrats at every turn. You have got to admit some of these things are really good ideas and the Democrats are the ones saying NO. The problem really is not Health Care but the Health Care Insurance costs. The health care insurance costs are the problem because of the Lawyers suing for every dime they can get. Not one of these ideas that the Republican party has come up with are in this 2,000 + page Healthcare bill, so how is this a bi-partisan bill, this is just an attempt to grab 1/6th of the private sectors economy. Where will they go from here, inspect your home to make sure it is safe for you and your children; this will turn into an intrusion of your civil liberties. If we do not get this changed you will pay later.

- Illegal aliens get insurance now when they go to a hospital, because hospitals will not turn you away if you have no insurance. What am I saying is; do not declare amnesty for illegal aliens they already get medical care, if you declare amnesty for citizenship there will be 100's charging the border to get amnesty.

- This bill would eliminate competition, just think about that. If you have to pay for the public option any way, why would you pay these extra taxes and then pay for your insurance as well. I have heard these taxes our estimated at $2,000.00 to $7,000.00 a year or about $180.00 to $520.00 a month extra in your taxes. When everybody is on the public option, not just the 46 million that they say have no insurance, then how much will your taxes go up then. This just takes competition out of our economy. Any person with common sense can see this happening.

- This bill does have an end of life counseling. The democrats behind this bill say that you need to consult with your doctor. That is true, but there should not be a third person in the room that represents the government or the person that pays for your health care. If you need a third person it should be a spouse, relative or close personal friend. So this is a death panel, call it what you want.

- Health care rationing already exists in this administration. The writing is on the wall. The

Obama children did not become vaccinated right away because this administration was exaggerating the Swine flu crisis, to push their health care agenda, and to help push their communist/socialist agenda's. Look at swine flu, only certain people get the shots and the government decides who will get those shots, will that be you or someone else. There weren't enough doses of the swine flu because our government wanted them processed in individual doses instead of a vial of 5-10 doses and it is easier to produce mass doses in a vial. Did the administration do this to create a bigger crisis and help push their Health Care Bill if a crisis actually happened? It was rather warm this November, do you think that might have been divine intervention to decrease the spread of the swine flu. The Swine Flu is a decease that takes large numbers of children's lives. So it is dangerous, but what if it was a real crisis and children were dieing everywhere, is this kind of health care you want. This administration needs to bud out and let the medical field care for this country; they are doing a pretty good job. *What if you lost a son or a daughter, or god forbid all of your children? If you think about it, this administration is not capable of handling a real crisis.* This should prove to you that this administration is out for **more government control** and not a real concern for your welfare. If you don't believe that, how about breast cancer. I am a man and even I know that early detection; something the health care industry has been harping on for years; is the best defense against breast cancer. It not only saves women's lives, because it stops cancer from spreading into the lungs, heart and brain, but early detection can also save the breast and allow a woman to retain her physical appearance and mental dignity. If you are not already seeing this as a BAD bill you need to wake up.

• Many doctors do drug test studies, this is where many drugs get approved by our government. Something that is already on the market or a drug from abroad gets its approval. People who have a certain affliction are asked to participate in a study. So many people in the study get the drug and then so many people get a placebo. Side effects are recorded and any health benefits are also recorded and if it does what it is supposed to do then the drugs get approved by the DEA and the drug is marketed. The whole while you are under the care of a physician. A good technique to approve drugs. Good doctors make more money for these kinds of drug tests they write papers and become published in their field. Large amounts of knowledge can be acquired from these drug studies. Do you think the smartest doctors will do this without any notoriety or monetary compensation? Will they continue to strive for excellence if not rewarded with at least notoriety? Some will continue, but many doctors will not even stay in the medical field.

• They tell me Medicare is broken. Well I say let's just fix Medicare and stop taking Medicare money from seniors health care to put into this public option bill, I mean this bill will not rebuild heath care and it will cost more.

- Illegal aliens get health care in our country now but this president wants to give them amnesty and make them citizens. It is true many Mexicans would love to live in this country just for our health care system. If you have a heart you don't blame them for wanting this, but if you have a reasonable mind you known we can't afford to help millions more. It is the cost of health care that we have to get under control. States near the border of Mexico now care for these illegal aliens and they pay higher local taxes then the rest of us to pay for these illegal aliens Medical Care.

- There are secret meetings or deals in the white house. After these deals the drug companies are behind this bill, not only are they behind this bill but the drug companies actually run advertisements for the health care bill? The pharmaceutical companies think they are not going to be hurt by this health care bill. If the government takes over the medical care in this country, at a later date they will take over the pharmaceutical companies. So why are they running adds for this health care bill. What could Obama have promised them to make them believe it was good for them to run adds for the Health Care bill.

- Why is AARP behind this bill when there are cuts to both Medicare and Medicaid, when the majority of their clientele are all over 55 years of age? If this is true seniors will be almost completely cared for by the government option.

When Medicare first came out it was very scary, but now seniors need Medicare and Medicaid so seniors need to be scared again. So why AARP is behind this new bill is it because they have the biggest gap insurance program in the United States? That is a very capitalist view, so I guess capitalism is alive. Again AARP should wake up because at a later date some president will say I think we should take over Gap insurance because we can run it better than AARP.

- Why is the American Medical Association (AMA) behind this bill? It is because any time you propose something you are going to have some people for it and some people against it. The AMA is only a 17% representation of Doctors. You can say anything no matter how bizarre and you will always be able to find some organization for it.

- Did you know this bill has fines for uninsured people? There are fines and they are over $2,000.00 for the fine. If you can't afford insurance do you think you will be able to pay for the fine?

- Then if you don't pay for the fine there is actually jail time in this bill if you are found guilty. In fact the president was asked about this on Meet the Press and he said nobody gets a free ride. I wonder how Obama supporters like that answer.

- Death panels do exist even if you call them end of life counseling, come on end of life equals Death, panels equals you, your doctor, and at least one government representative deciding if this is a <u>financially</u> sound decision.

- Paid abortions, no matter how they try to hide it abortions are paid for by your taxes.
- This bill has paid abortions, end life counseling (Government controlled youth in Asia) so what is next destruction of life that isn't perfect like downs syndrome, or something else that is an inconvenience, or maybe stopping pregnancies that have cycle cell anemia, aides/HIV or something that will take a great deal care after birth, anything not quite normal. There is a movie about this, a futuristic movie where only 1 in a hundred births are allowed because those are the only ones worth saving, the rest are not perfect. Is that the direction we are headed.
- I heard that there is a clause in this bill that allows no private insurance after 2013, after the reelection of Obama; he would not care what you think after another term in office. Maybe the money that they collect on the Medical Care Bill before the health care actually begins will go into the slush fund that was created with this stimulus package.
- Why would any bill take almost 2,000 pages to explain unless there are things hidden in this bill?

The President of the Harvard school of medicine said 2 things about what was real in this bill. The first thing is the Actual health care is good now and that will stay the same (but it will decline under this bill, because of less funds and more rationing) the second thing he talked about was the number that are covered, and he said that will increase because people will see it as being free.

The Democrats are planning to get $500 billion from Medicare and increase the coverage to people age 55. So they are going to have more people covered and less money to do it with. The original number of people who did not have health insurance was 47/49 million, something like that. With this new bill from Harry Reed the cost will be 2.5 trillion dollars and there will still be 24 million uninsured, and then having fines for uninsured people. None of this makes any sense does it?

SUMMARY

In chapter VI, I wrote about some of the good Ideas that the Republicans had about trying to save our health care system and how the Democrats call us the no party, because they claim we say no to everything they do. The real problem is that the Democrats Health Care Bill is a partisan Health Care Bill and the Democrats have said no to several very good ideas to fix the health insurance problem. I like being called the party of <u>KNOW</u>.

You <u>KNOW</u>; WE HAVE THE GREATEST HEALTH CARE SYSTEM IN THE WORLD!

Chapter VII
Leftovers

This Chapter will jump around allot because I will be covering a lot of little areas.

Religion & Hope are the first things in this chapter. I will talk about God and my religious teachings and the hope you should have for our great nation. I hope I will give you hope to believe in America the way I do. I have already given you embargos to follow and if you believe in America and the constitution of the United States of America you will follow these embargos. I sincerely believe that we need to take back our country in a peaceful manner.

The first thing that I want to say is that **my religious leaders** were not strong enough. When I was a kid if I would have told my mom that I was a pro choice person she would have put her hands on her head and said "Oh my God, I going to church to say a rosary for you". This was my mom's way of telling me I need to go to church and pray. Let me explain how easy this is. When you have a debate you have a pro side and a con side.

PRO CHOICE (the choice of keeping a pregnancy to full term or aborting a pregnancy)

CON CHOICE (the choice of no choice, or a full term pregnancy and having a baby)

PRO LIFE (being for the birth in every circumstance)

CON LIFE (being against birth in every case)

Obviously the pro choice people would not take the con life side but no matter how you look at it they are against life, because an abortion stops a pregnancy and a baby from coming into this world. You can say you're not killing a baby because you call it a fetus, but to me you are killing a baby. This is very simple if you have an abortion you will not have a baby, but if you do not have an abortion you will have a baby. Stopping a baby from being born is a death! This is really sad because if you were to talking about hurting somebody's pet your neighborhood would want you ridden out of town on a rail. But stopping a human life is O.K. and the truth again, if you do NOT have an abortion you will have a baby. When you use simple terms, decisions are simple. You can call it a fetus all you want but you are stopping a baby from being born.

The pro choice side of this issue wants you to take into consideration, that when abortions were illegal these abortions were being done in back dimly lighted alleyways, by people who were not doctors and this was dangerous. That is true, because **abortions were illegal**. They want you to believe that if a women is raped or where an act of incest was committed and a pregnancy followed, that this was bad. I agree that these things are bad, but most abortions today are not being done for those 2 reasons. When I was in college a college friend of mine told me that her girlfriend already had 3 abortions and her friend was only 21. Many young women are using abortions as a birth control device, and that is even worse then when abortions were illegal. Abortions are now being done because it is a bad time for this woman to be pregnant. Maybe she's too young or we are not financially ready when the truth is that this child is an inconvenience. I'm sorry but even when your ready and financially sound a child it is still an inconvenience. Why do we have children? When they do something horrible wrong like poor bleach on the rug and you are ready to scream at them and they look up at you with that impish smile and all you can do is laugh or hug them or something like that, all material things no longer matter because you love them. That is an inconvenience, so I don't care how much you plan your pregnancy and your life, children are an inconvenience and they are worth every bit of it.

So why do I start like this, because of two reasons! The first reason is that I am going to blame the American Counsel of Catholic Bishops, because they let this get out of hand. The Catholic Church, when I was a kid would have; excommunicated you; kicked you out of the Catholic Church for doing something like proclaiming to be pro choice. This was just unheard of when I was a kid and at the very least they would not have allowed you to go to communion while you were in this state of sin. You would have to go to confession and confess your sins before you would have been given communion. As a politician if you continued to <u>proclaim</u> your pro-choice status and you are doing that by proclaiming that on your web site and then claiming that you are a catholic. This insults the Catholic Church. Your local church must do the hard truth, and ask you if you are still pro-choice. If you answer yes, then you need to be excommunicated, because that is Catholicism, this is a church issue not a civil matter. The problem is that proclaiming Pro-Choice puts you in a state of sin so you can not continue to say you are a Catholic. I do believe in separation of church and state and that is why you can not tell the world that you are Catholic and be pro-choice. Senator Kennedy was allowed to proclaim Pro-choice for years and was still allowed to be a Catholic. I am saying this needs to stop going on. Now I understand many of you think a great deal of Senator Kennedy. I just want this, I am a Catholic and pro-choice status to be discontinued. These are the teachings of my church and they should be enforced no matter who you are. I don't mean to disgrace Senator Kennedy's name in a derogatory manner, but these are the teachings of the Catholic Church and the need to be enforced. Senator John Kerry also proclaims that he is Pro-Choice and proclaims that he is a Catholic. This as a Catholic offends me and there are many politicians that do this. He should be excommunicated from the Catholic Church if he does not confess his sins for being pro-choice and switch to pro-life and ask for forgiveness. This I am sorry to say is the fault of the Catholic Bishops for not enforcing this part of Catholicism.

People who are for this health care bill believe that the government should take care of those who can not take care of themselves. I do not believe that paying for legalized abortions is caring for those who can not take care of themselves; in fact it seems like the opposite. I don't believe that I should have to pay for abortions when I do not morally agree with abortions. We continue to take this <u>unalienable right for life</u> out of the constitution with this new Public Health Care Bill. The government is about to decide what health care you can have, so maybe Youth in Asia is the next thing to be added to the Health Care Bill. It might take 10 years, but this maybe next. After that the Government may decide to change the Health Care Bill by using ultrasounds to decide what birth defects you can deliver into this world or what birth defects you can not deliver into this world, because it is too costly to care for children with disabilities. I am worried about where this bill can go by adding to this Health Care Bill in years to come, I see bad things coming if it passes. The congress said itself that this is not a mansion, it is a starter home. Which means in years to come many of the things that I have suggested will come true.

You may feel that we have no hope, cheer-up we can do things right now, like embargos, join me. Another thing we are going to do, if you start a business. Try to find a way to put the word conservative, or the word republic or just the word TEA in the name in your business and the Tea Party people and the readers of this book the conservatives of this nation will support your business. This is going to be our code, through the words republic or conservative or tea.

Another Democratic concept is the use of embryos for stem cell research; this is the stupidest thing I have ever heard of. The umbilical cord has thousands of Stem cells in it, just ask any Obstetrician. So if you want to do research with these stem cells you would have more stem cells in multiple umbilical cords than you would to get from one embryo because The stem cells in an embryo are already starting to change into brain cells and muscle cells and bone cells and heart cells and so on and there are 1,000's of births daily that you could use stemm cells from umbilical cords. How can the people who work for Obama in the medical field be so uninformed about stemm cells? Why is it that people who have cycle cell anemia in their family history don't know that freezing that umbilical cord could save there child's life at a later time in their child's life, if they come down with cycle cell anemia? They would literally have there own cells and would not need blood transfusions or bone marrow transfers.

Another thing that needs to be talked about is ACORN; many of us already know they are dirty just for taking federal money and supporting the Democratic Party. Their funds should be cut off or they should not be allowed to give money to one party without giving the equal amount of money to the other party. In this manner we give acorn federal money and they give the money to the Democratic Party. I pay taxes, so a portion of my taxes supported Obama, which is definitely not what I wanted. When I pay my taxes and I am a republican it should not go to the Democratic Party. Every person alive should be able to see how that stinks. It just violates fair business practices no matter how you look at it. So if you are a conservative you should stop any activity with ACORN. So this is your next embargo. **7. Stop any business dealings with ACORN.**

Still another thing that needs to be talked about is that this Congress gives itself and the federal government a 3% pay raise when the rest of the country is in a recession. I was in the Army when Ronald Regan was President of this country and one year we did not receive a pay raise. Think about this the Army is about 400,000 strong, the Navy is over 300,000 strong and the Air Force and the Marines are well over 300,000 strong. That is 1 million people plus. Say that 3% is $30.00 per person and I know it is a lot more than $30.00 a person. Now let's add in the Cost Guard & Department the interior the Department of Natural Resources and DEA and all federal jobs. Just the military is a $30 million dollar pay raise. That is right just the military, but this pay raise goes to all federal employees. You are looking at maybe as much as 1-2 hundred million dollars.

If you have an insurance policy of any kind or if you have any kind of financial investments in AIG close out your accounts. If you're a CEO of a company or a corporation and you have any kind of insurance or any kinds of investments in AIG close your accounts out. This is our next embargo

8. Stop any financial investment in A.I.G., cancel your insurance with them and move it to a new company. Conservatives that manage corporations stop any corporate investments in A.I.G., and cancel any insurance your company has and move it to a new company.

9. If you have any financial investments or insurance with any Bank that took TARP funds and has not repaid them yet like Bank of America or Citicorp or any other bank that has taken Tarp funds and has not yet repaid that TARP money. Make sure that they have outstanding TARP loans with the government first. I want you to close out your accounts and place them with other companies.

We do not need to pay these two institutions when the government is already using our money to support these companies without taxpayer approval. We have to stick together and hurt these liberal programs. This is still a free country and we have the right to spend our money where we want to, and invest it with whom we want to invest with. All you have to do is to ask the banks if they have any TARP money and if they have repaid those TARP loans.

Global warming is still another thing that needs to be written about; they say that crop production will go down as the heat continues to increase. Do you remember how I told you that in California a huge number of farms that are not being irrigated by a damn to protect the smelt? No farm produce proves global warming, is this also a part of this conspiracy. Do you think they are going to try to use that as proof of global warming? How stupid do they think we are? This smells like a huge conspiracy. Why is the mass media not looking into this, this just sounds like a government conspiracy?

Still another item that needs to be written about is the way our Constitution works; it is really hard to have more than two major groups in competition for these presidential positions. Especially with the Electoral College being in place, Sarah Palin understands this; I know this because she said she would support whoever gets the Republican Presidential nomination. If you were around a few years back a man named Ross Perot ran for office of President and he really did split the Republican Party, so much so that the Democrats won the Election. Mr. Perot had a lot of conservative ideas and made good of sense. He was a businessman and was going to run the Federal government like a business. Make no mistake about this, he was a real candidate for president, and he split our party. This business like approach makes so much sense that he had a lot of followers.

Our problem in the last election was a lot of things; one was that John McCain was too old to sway the younger voters that were Independents or the undecided at that time. Another thing was that he was smart, but for years we have been beat up about we how need to be bi-partisan. Now that the Democrats control the congress <u>they are not allowing republican ideas and opinions whatsoever,</u> where did that bi-partisan reasoning go now that they are in charge. So the states that can vote in the primary for our candidate please do not elect an older candidate. I live in a state that does not vote in the primary in time to sway our party for our candidate. I would like Huckabee to be our candidate, but I would <u>gladly </u>support Palin, Romney, or Palantee. Right now these are the four people who seem to be getting ready for a presidential race. I would also like to see Sarah Palin as the Vice President, because I believe that after 8 years she could still run a presidential campaign that would win. That would give us 8 years, followed by another 8 years and as bad as this situation is, we may need 16 years to fix our government. Glen Beck is one of the best investigative correspondents I have ever seen, and I do not mean to bad mouth him, but something I just can not agree with is this third party crap. I have just stated what I feel to be the truth and there are 2 things I do not like about him. During this last election he actually said on the radio, now that McCain is the Republican candidate he did not know who he was going to vote for. I am a Republican first and a conservative second, so I was offended by that statement, I will not vote for a conservative candidate in our next presidential election unless he is running on the Republican ticket. So if you can not convert the Conservative Party into our Republican party you will lose my vote. I will not vote for a Conservative Party until it is a proven party. You can complain about the Republicans, but every one of them voted against this medical health care bill. Even Olympia Snow! This is not how you support your party, but you see Glen Beck wants to have a third party with some substance, well I am sorry, but this is not what we need right now, because a real conservative would not even consider voting for a democrat like Barrack Obama. So Barrack Obama becoming president is at least a little bit Glenn Beck's fault. I mean if a man like Glenn Beck with all of his listeners. If ¼ of his listeners vote for Obama, that can be a lot of votes. No real conservative would have ever voted for Obama. Another thing that I do not like about Glen beck is that he uses scares tactics when he reports what he uncovers.

I saw a survey on Fox News that showed this break down of how the party break down would work be if we Added a conservative party right now and it looks like this:

-Democrats 36%
-Conservatives 23%

-Republicans 18%
-Undecided 28 %

I am afraid of this conservative movement because it is very attractive to the republicans. Just like when Ross Perot ran, he split the Republican Party because a large number of republicans love the idea of a balanced budget and run the country like a business, the democrats and liberals do not see this as a big deal so they would not change their democratic vote. So you lose Republican votes for this conservative movement, but very little votes from the Democratic Liberal Party. The problem is that if you split the Republican Party you let the Democratic Party Win again and then we have 8 years of Obamanomics to fix. You would need to win almost the entire undecided vote to lock down a win; we can not afford another 4 years of Obamanomics. The ideas of Barrack Obama winning a second term by it self should scare you enough to fix the Republican Party and not start a new Conservative Party. At this time in our history we can not take that chance of losing this next presidential election. If we merge the conservatives into the Republican Party we only needs to get 9% of the 28% of the undecided vote to win the presidency think about that only 9%. I am sorry but we need a lock in this next election

I know that Glen Beck would like this third party of Conservatives, but here is the problem. If these liberals and democrats say that they are conservatives and then turn there back on us the true Conservatives, all that happens is that you split the Republican Party again. Look at all of the Democratic senators that said they would not vote for this Medical Care Bill and then voted for it anyway. I do not want to put my faith in a group of people that change there vote so easily. If they don't change there vote like they said they would then you don't have a chance of winning the next election and you are stuck with Obamamanomics maybe for life. We will not be able to change these communist/socialism agendas after being set in place for 8 years. We will have another 4 years of Obama and his communist/socialist government and we will not be able to reverse some of these communist bills that our being instituted in our government right now. Take the Health care Bill for example, in the next 2 elections if we rebuilt our Republican Party, before the health care bill takes hold and we take a majority in the house and the congress and we can vote the medical care bill out by repealing it and pass some of the things that would really help the Heath Insurance Industry and the capitalism in this country that makes smart dedicated people stay in the medical industry. I like my doctor and I want to keep him. Another thing I do not want is some liberal government representative involved in my medical care decisions. Also to keep other things like a medical savings plan, competition across state lines, tax deductions for doctor visits when seeing the uninsured, and tax deferred items for the uninsured, the most important of all is TORT REFORM and insurance industry requirements to reduce costs since tort reform will be started for the medical industry. I just heard about a lawsuit case on the radio where the victim was awarded 26 Million dollars, I wonder how much the lawyer got. Have you ever noticed all of the lawsuits against certain drugs on TV, this country is really getting out of hand. The lawyers love to sue the hospitals because they know they have a lot of money and they are insured heavily. Why do lawyers deserve so much of the lawsuit? With all the talk about how much a professional athlete makes, why do lawyers make so much?

Now after all this talk just about the new medical bill we will probably be supporting the Emperor of the world Barrack Obama and eventually his World medical program. We will be paying our Carbon footprint taxes so that they can have the redistribute of wealth. Then Obama will say something like this 1 dollar for Africa, 1 dollar for South America, 1 dollar for Europe, 1 dollar for Asia and 1 dollar for me. Countries like Russia and China and the rich Oil Countries won't be paying this tax because for some reason they are considered as developing nations when they loan us money, figure that one out that is right we will be giving them even more money not just the interest on our loans. So who is paying the majority of the bill, America? Like Glenn Beck this should scare you half to death, it scares me.

When I was in the military, I went to one of my platoon sergeants with a problem and he said to me, "If you don't have a solution for the problem you're bringing to me, shut up." Ever since then I try to suggest things that might work instead of the way they are. You do that, the same way a think tank works or brainstorming. You have a problem, then everyone in the think tank offers a solution and then you chop up each others ideas until you find a solution that works. If my book sells, I will write another book with more and better questions to ask your next elected officials and offer solutions to many of the situations that this administration has intensified or created. I have about 5 solutions that will create revenue some by tax cuts and a couple of ideas to heal this economy and I will explain how they work. All but one of these will increase revenues. I have 3 different ideas as to how to pay off our national deficit. I have different ideas for how to pay for medical care for the uninsured even with existing conditions.

I know it seems like I am jumping around to a lot of different ideas in this chapter and I am but that is because this is the section where I write about a lot of things. There is an organization called askheritage.org that is asking for donations, heritage.com is a think tank that is working out issues with the constitution of the United States keeping in mind legislation that is being proposed. I am <u>not</u> affiliated with this organization in any way and I am only plugging for them because I believe in the things they write.

SUMMARY

In chapter VII, I talked about my religion and how The American Counsel of Bishops let me down by allowing politicians to proclaim their Pro-Choice label and allow them to receive communion and stay Catholic. How I believe that no matter how you look at it if you have an abortion you are at the very least stopping a life from being born, it is that simply to me.

Chapter VIII
Conservative Democrats and Independents

First of all, I want to thank all of the Conservative Democrats and the Conservative Independents. You are the same as us the Conservative Republicans. We want a balanced budget, reasonable taxes and the way of life we grew up with. We have to defeat this liberal socialist Administration that is taking over our government; they are trying to take us from a Republic to a socialist Government. We will not be able to stop this socialist movement without you the Democratic conservatives and the Independent conservatives. I wrote about this earlier in this book. We need to back the Republican Party in the Presidential election for 2 reasons. The first reason is that the Republican Party is voting no against every bill the Democrats try to pass them. They are not doing this for spite, but because the Republicans in this first year have seen that this Administration does not want to be bi-partisan and because the agendas that are being pushed are socialist. Without the Republicans in congress this is just whitewash. The second reason is that we might not be able to defeat the Liberals in 2010 and 2012 as conservatives alone. We will need the Republican Party, because we not take the chance of Obamanomics going past 2010, we must vote them out of office in the 2010 election, and win the majority. Do not buy into this health care bill stuff. If the republicans had a say in this conversion between senate Health Care bill and the house Health Care bill it would be better, but it will never really help our country.

I am hoping that the thought of President Obama and his Administration running this country for 8 years would be scary enough for you to vote republican. We need to restore capitalism and save our economy, with some economic enticements. Like I said it is not hard to fix this economy, but this Administration is a bunch of theorists and have no real ideas among them, which is weird because it really is actually very easy to fix this economy with very simple ideas.

All of us just want the same thing. I said it before; we just want life easier for our kids than life was for us. There is no difference if you are a Democrat, Republican, Independent or even a liberal when it comes to our kids. This Administration wants a Medical Health care bill that will cost us 5% more in our taxes, maybe anther 5% in cap and trade. Most American Families can not afford a 1% pay raise in our taxes, much less a 10% plus raise in our taxes.

If this government accepts this New World Order, how much will that cost in American taxes? I heard President Obama say at the conference in Copenhagen that he wanted to commit 100 BILLION dollars and I don't know if that was a year, 1 time or what. Then later I heard him say he wanted to give 1 billion dollars a year for 30 years. I guess you have to listen to fox news to hear these kinds of things. I do not believe that this part of his speech was shown on any other channels. This commitment was shot down because a Republican told the Climate Change Group that President Obama could not make that decision alone and that it would have to ratified by ¾ of congress.

The Climate change people are a funny group of people. There are over 140 private jets, and well over 2,000 limousines needed to accommodate the Climate Change people going to Copenhagen, I wonder what kind of a carbon footprint that causes. Ironic isn't it that the people most worried about carbon footprint and emissions are doing all of this polluting to stop pollution. The climate change people could have done all of this as a computer conference instead of taking all of these private jets and limos. I wonder how many of us were noticing this like I was.

I understand now that this Administration is going to take 500 billion out of Medicare and expand the coverage to people 55 years of age. They are going to use less money to cover more people, I wonder how that is going to work. They say Medicare is broken, if it is broken how come it has 500 billion dollars that it can spare and still cover more people. I am good at math usually, but this is one problem I can not figure out, it must be that new modern math.

If this Administration allows the New World Order to give us a new monetary system for our dollar, I wonder who will benefit from that. Will we be able to purchase gas for the same price as we do now? When the middle class and upper class go overseas will our dollar still give us the purchasing power that we have now? I wonder if as many college kids that go on Spring Break to Cancun in Mexico will have to pay more money then they used to.

These are the things that the conservatives do not want changed. I do believe these changes could be coming. That is why we are going to use the Embargos in Appendix A to fight these liberals now. We will do this until we can vote them out of office in 2010 and 2012. If you save money by using these embargos, you can put into a fund for you to back your conservative congressman. What is really funny is that if this Administration passes all of the liberal bills it will have to raise taxes, and it will force lower class people in this nation to follow these embargos anyway, because allot of these embargos are the lower classes luxuries. Now we are volunteering to do these embargos, and later on we will be forced into these embargos.

The way this Administration closes doors and has conferences, then opens doors and Senator Landrieu from Louisiana leaves and has 300 million dollars for her state and then she votes a certain way. A certain way that she did not vote before, makes it look like her vote was bought. That just <u>sounds like a bribe</u> to me, Chicago Style Politics. I wonder if we were to stand outside of the voting booths and we were to offer people $100.00 if they voted for the Republican Canidate instead of Barrack Obama if that would be legal to buy their votes. Why are ethics of the Americans people expected to be different then Ethics of our politicians in Washington?

Kathleen Sabilious said a portion of the money to pay for the health care bill is **NOT** earmarked for the health care bill. Where is it going, into the Presidents slush fund? None of the things that are being reported to us on fox news is being reported on the other networks. These things do not seem to make any sense and yet no other channel is showing these things, but it does seem to make sense.

Why is our President working so hard to stop the coal industry? Coal is dirty so it must be stopped. Does our President just want more people out of work? Miners of the coal will be out of work. More truckers will be out of work. The Green jobs do not last, and there are not as many green jobs. This is another thing that this Administration is doing that does not make any sense. How many ways have I suggested in this book that this Administration has created unemployment, it just seems like this Administration is trying to stop jobs, I wonder if crime is going up or down? I would like to see those stats, but that is not being report on.

So our next embargo is from a suggestion by, Jason Lewis who is one of the talk show hosts here, he said if you don't like the colleges you can stop giving to them. So let us the Conservatives stop donating to the colleges. This will show the Liberals we are a force to be reckoned with, if you are a conservative Catholic and you donate to Notre Dame please send them a note with your next donation and tell them if they ever have a commencement speaker again that is a pro-choice, who is a political speaker or otherwise, that you will never send them another donation. This is a Catholic College, and as a Catholic College you should be ashamed to have even had the thought of a pro-choice speaker. The old priest that was on your campus praying for those pro-choice none believers, should not have been escorted off of your campus, he is a man of the cloth. I hope god can forgive you.

Our last embargo is to, give no money to the Sierra Club because they are Liberals and backers of this Global Warming agenda and they are all Liberals.-Show this Administration we know who you liberals are and we will not support this kind of socialist agenda's anymore.

Californian's where is Pelosi with this smelt minnow crisis. Everything in this Administration is a crisis. She is one of the big dogs in congress and she gets money for the frogs around San Francisco bay, she may have even helped the smelt get put on the endanger species list. The farmers are being foreclosed on and the farm workers and some of crop pickers are out of work. Californians are losing jobs while the fertile valleys of California are drying up, what is this Administration doing to help?

Arnold Schwartzneiger is trying to get stimulus money for a canal, while the second in command in congress Pelosi lets California dry up. Where is the stimulus money for the canal, to be honest with you I don't think the canal would be a good Idea because it is too expensive, but Pelosi got California stimulus money to help the frogs; did it create jobs or help the farmers? Pelosi is your Senator; you would think that she would want to help her constituents, especially the farmers, isn't that what DFL stands for, it's OK because she made sure that there wasn't a tax on botox. All across America there are foreclosures, if America had more jobs do you think there would be as many foreclosures. Your Senator should be creating jobs for Californian's. You should think about getting you a new Congress woman. She seems more interested in keeping the wrinkles out of her face, and then she does about the California farmers.

Another thing with our economy getting so bad is the fact that now gas prices are going up. If you're wondering why the gas prices are going up? It is simple, these oil countries see us owing the Chinese and printing money and more money and deflating our dollar to a point that they need to make more money to make the same money they made 6 months ago. How much more will we have to pay these oil companies in the future? Would these oil prices go down if we had another place to get it, like drilling off our own coastlines? We would be creating a back-up supply and then we would actually have some negotiating power with these people.

This Democratic Liberal government wants you to believe in this Carbon Footprint stuff. If you watched star trek, there was a movie where the enterprise had to go back to earth and save the whales. At one point they needed money, but the concept of money had not been in their society for years. Maybe the Democrats watched that movie and thought that is how we will run the world with carbon credits. This is made up futuristic concepts. Something will always back our money. Star trek is a fictional series.

When you become a conservative you realize that there must be something behind your money some kind of value. Now we say my house is worth $200,000.00, if we do not change this maybe in 50 years we will be saying my house is worth 4,000 carbon credits. That concept is very scary to me.

SUMMARY

In chapter VIII, I wrote about how I am very grateful that many Independents and Democrats are joining us in a push for conservatism. I also said that Obama and his Administration are a bunch of theorists.

Book Conclusion

The thing that I want to express first and foremost is that this is not a book based on factual detail. For the most part, almost every thing in this book is my opinion based on my own personal experience of life. Yet every day I find that these opinions are also the opinions of many main stream hard working Americans. Many Americans see this as a liberal socialist movement, and we do not like this movement, I feel very strongly about this. This is a very real problem. Many Americans feel the same way I do and really HATE the direction our country is moving. We feel our country is moving toward socialism and this is unacceptable to us. So in this book I have proposed ways that we can fight this socialist movement in a peaceful, civil way. The other way is to violently rebel, and I am not condoning that. I have made some accusations in this book which are pure speculation of motives regarding the liberal agendas of this Administration, and on the basis of what we are hearing about this government they are very reasonable accusations.

What you need to remember about this book, is to identify in you own mind whether the Presidents ambitions are what I said or otherwise, are they good for our America. I still think he will have a run at Emperor of the world at one point or another. I also believe now because of Copenhagen that he will not achieve what my vision of his dream is, at least not until a <u>much</u> later global warming conference.

Most important next is to vote Republican at least for the presidential election, because of what I stated earlier in this book about the votes of the electoral college and what I am going to say again.

Most important of all in this book I want you to remember Perot. Remember Ross Perot! Let's start to say "Remember Perot". This is the break down of how the American people feel about their party affiliation. These numbers were on fox news as of November.

-Democrats 36%
-Conservatives 23%
-Republicans 18%
-Undecided 28 %

I am afraid of this conservative movement only because it is very attractive to the Republicans. Just like when Ross Perot ran for president, he split the Republican Party because a large number of Republicans love the idea of a balanced budget and the Democrats and Liberals do not seem to care as much about a balanced budget so they will not change their party affiliation from the Democratic Party. So we will lose many Republican votes to this conservative movement, but very few votes from the Democratic Liberal Party. The problem is that you may split the Republican Party and you will let the Democratic Party win again. Then we will have 8 years of Obama because the Republican Party gets split again. We would need to win almost the entire undecided vote to lock down a win, and we can not afford another 4 years of Obama style of Government. So the idea of Barrack Obama winning a second term by it self should scare you enough to fix the Republican Party and not start a new Conservative Party. If we do it my way and merge the conservatives into the Republican Party we only need to get 9% out of the 28% of the undecided vote to win the presidency. This could be a landslide at least a much easier battle to win. Now after we win the Presidential election in 2012 and defeat this socialist movement if the new incumbent President wants to run his/her second term campaign on the Conservative Party ticket I have no problem with that, I am only worried about now the next presidential election.

Look at all of the Democratic senators that said they would <u>not </u>vote for this Medical Care Bill and then did anyway. We need to depend on the Republicans and have the conservatives join-in with us for at least this Presidential election and then you can try to make a conservative party. This next Presidential election is Vital for the freedoms of our country.

Every chapter goes through some things these liberals are doing, and how these embargos hurt these liberals. So use the quick list of embargos to feel like you are doing something now. Part of the liberal agenda is to say something enough times and eventually it becomes true even if it started out as a complete lie. Look at President Clinton and his affair, at first he denied it, once it was proved true he kept saying it for awhile, but then it was O.K., no ethics violation, just a thing every man does. So the liberals have been denying the fact that these Global Warming temperatures were falsified. Now in a couple of months or so they will start to say its ok if the temperatures are not exactly right. <u>It is not ok to falsify this information,</u> because when it is the empirical information to prove your theory. So now there is absolutely no substance to anything they say because it was probably falsified. So this is another thing that the liberals say that is not true and then eventually you let up or start to believe that there isn't anything that you can do about it. Do not let up on this, this is a course of action that we must stay vigilant at, because if we let up on this, this socialism will control us.

When people say that the Republicans are the same as the Democrats, no they are not. In fact they seem to be completely opposite. Other than Olympia Snow on that first stimulus vote the Republicans have been against everything that the Democrats have been for. In fact they have had to buy some of those Democrats votes to pass these really bad bills. Some of these Democrats had to be bought with money for their states by their own party to vote a certain way. How bad is something if your own party has to coerce you with money for your state to pas a bill?

I have mentioned many things this Administration is doing that are causing people to lose their jobs. If they take over the Medical Care Industry many insurance agents will be out of work they will not all be hired by the Government and then there will be lines at the hospitals just like at the DMV. Take the coal industry, put some coal plants out of business, and you put their employees out of work, the coal miners out of work, truckers that haul the coal, you are hurting the trains that transport coal, and more truckers on the delivery of the coal. Let's not forget the Farmers in California, and the farm hands and the truckers that haul the produce to market and again the trains to other parts of the country, and truckers that deliver produce on the other end. All of these people are or will be put out of work during a time when our country is in a recession.

These theorists in Washington our really hurting us, I heard crime is going up. I really wonder if crime is up. The problem is we are still hearing that this is Bush's fault. President Bush has not been in office for over a year, take the blame, it is your America. With more taxes on our fuel and the deflation of the dollar overseas, it will cost more because America moves on gas in our cars. Even when we start to import Chinese vegetables there will be a lot more costs, you will be paying overseas shipping costs American truckers American trains, and again American delivery truckers. Gas will be more because of cap and trade and no offshore exploration to try to balance the cost of gas. Utilities will also be going up because of cap and trade, so it will cost us more to live, not to mention Medical care bill costing us a 5% increase on our taxes or more, and that will go up every year with more and more people being put on the public option. Small businesses will be going under because they will not be able to afford the insurance (Public Option) costs.

It really is looking mighty gloomy unless we fight back now. These embargos will stop the liberals from donating so much to these campaigns and we will be hurting their pocket book. This will show the liberals that we have a voice and then we will vote them out of office. God help us.

This book is meant to be a how to book for us conservatives, to strike these liberals back with embargos before we vote them out of office. I intend to write another book to show how easy it is to restore our capitalistic economy and help set our country back on a prosperous path by showing this government how to create jobs, because that is the real key. I will do this by telling my opinions as what bills we need passed and what should be in them and lastly who to vote for by way of our values and not by whom they are or what they say. Lastly I will voice my thoughts about the reformation of the Republican Party!

Questions for your Congressmen

When you vote for a congressman he/she should willing to do certain things to work for you and get your vote. These are the questions you should ask him and look for exact answers; politicians do not seem to answer the question when they answer questions. Most politicians seem to ramble. That crap needs to stop as well.

These are the minimums;

1. Are you willing to give the American people a balanced budget and take NO pay raises until this deficit is gone?
2. Bills should be about one subject with no riders; for example, no money for troubled schools on the same bill with for money for military equipment.
3. The declaration of independence needs to be read before every session of congress.
4. Your new congressman needs to believe this portion of the declaration of Independence, "…Governments are institutes among men,

deriving the just powers <u>from the consent of the government …</u>".

5. Are you willing to only do 3 terms as a Senator no more career politicians and would you be willing to write a bill stating this.

6. The new congressman should be willing to require the pledge of allegiance to be said before school everyday in elementary schools. The Declaration of Independence, the Constitution, the Bill of Rights, and the Gettysburg Address should be required to be read <u>aloud</u> in every American History class while in high school.

7. Would you write a bill limiting the amount of personal attendant the President and first person is allowed to have?

8. Would you write a bill to ban the Czars?

Some of the Veteran Democratic Congressmen are retiring. Do not be fooled by this move. They would have been beaten badly in an election, so the Democratic Party told them to retire; now so their replacements can say I would not have voted for the Health Care Bill or whatever other bills they may pass, maybe like cap and trade. Do not buy into this rhetoric, because they would have voted for it just like their predecessor. We need conservatives preferably republicans. The Republican congressmen are now standing strong in this troubling congress. They have done all the right things; remember they can not get any television coverage, because they are Republicans. So they can not tell you what they are doing or what is going on in congress. Do not lose faith in our Republican Senators and Congressmen.

Remember some of those ideas as to how to change the health insurance industry, they came from the Republicans that are in congress now. These same ideas were in bills proposed by Republicans. These bills were stopped because they were Republicans, and the Democratic majority did not let them get the votes to go in front of congress to even be discussed. Please believe me when I tell you that the Republican Congressmen are not the same as the Liberal Democratic Congressmen, they have learned allot about what the American people really want, they are listening, it is not the Republicans that are shutting off their phones, it is the Democratic Congressmen that are shutting off their phones.

Remember it was Pelosi that called us, the Tea Party people, Nazi's, when they Liberals are the ones that have the Socialist agenda's. I really believe that the Democratic Party thinks that we are stupid and this agenda is good for us so they are pushing it through anyway.

Do not forget Harry Reid, he is one of the big dogs in Washington, one of the main players in this socialist movement and Health Care Bill that most people do not want. Has Harry Reid really done anything for his constituents in Nevada? I do not know of any stimulus money he got for the state of Nevada and yet he is involved in the composition or helps compose many of these bills. Lastly why is this Health Care Bill so important and we hear so little about creating jobs. The people out of work do not believe that the recession is over and that the first stimulus package has already fixed our jobless rate.

Appendix A

The Quick list of hard choices!

EMBARGOS WE CAN USE NOW!

1. ***We will not attend any movies until we start to be heard, or at least until the 2010 elections.*-**This will show this Administrations that redistribution of wealth goes both ways so be careful.

2. ***We will not attend any Professional sporting events in the first two weeks of every month.*-** This will show this Administration that we will be heard no matter how hard you try to stifle us. By our empty seats at professional Sporting events we show this nation our strength because these games are nationally televised and probably liberal owned. This will also tell the mass media that we are being heard in the absence of our seats.

3. ***We are going to cancel all subscriptions to magazines and newspapers, except the wall street journal only if you need it for work.*-** This will show the mass media they are not in charge; we are. Liberals who own and direct these papers; take notice. Maybe the reason that newspapers are struggling is because you

no longer report both sides of the issues. You report all of the Democratic liberal stuff, but you need to print the other side of the issue. Look at the Global Warming issue, you do not even show the other side. If your paper goes under, understand that it is your fault, all the people want is unbiased reporting.

4. **We will only buy Ford, Saturn or American made cars only, no GM, Chrysler or foreign made cars.**-This will tell the President you should not be involved in the private sector in any way and until you get out of the private sector we will not buy anything from government owned companies. As the president you have no right to fire or require any private business to fire anyone.

5. **You like me, need to cancel your AARP insurance and membership.** This will show this Administration that when you close your doors and do something we do not like we are not going to accept this and maybe AARP will have to loose some business to realize that they are supposed to take care of our seniors not your business first. Your members are your business, wake up. There are other Gap insurances out there find one.

6. ***Stop any business dealings with ACORN***-This will show this Administration business with ACORN needs to stop.

7. **Stop any financial investments or any insurance policies with A.I.G. cancel those policies or accounts and move them to another company.**-This will show this Administration that we do not approve of

your saving companies with our taxes, or loans against our taxes.

8. **If you have any financial investments or insurances with any bank that has not repaid their TARP loans move those accounts and insurances to other companies, even if it is your home loans.** This will show this Administration that you are spending my money and I want it stopped. So move your accounts to Banking institutions that have already paid their TARP loans back. We do have a voice and we will be heard.

9. **On talk radio in Minnesota, Jason Lewis a talk show host said; if you don't like these colleges teaching these liberal ideas stop donating to them. So our 10**[th] **embargo is not to donate to your Alma matter.** This will show liberals we are a force to be reckoned with. If you are a conservative and you donate to Notre Dame, please send them a note with your next donation and tell them if they ever have a commencement ceremony speaker who is a pro-choice speaker, that you will never send them another donation. This is a Catholic College, and as a Catholic College you should be ashamed to have even had a thought to have a pro-choice speaker. Secondly, that old priest that was on your campus praying for those none believers, should not have been escorted off of your campus, he is a man of God. I hope God can forgive you.

10. *Give no money to the Sierra Club because they are liberals and big backers of this Global Warming agenda and they are all*

> *liberals.*-Tell this Administration that we know where many of you liberals work.
>
> 11. **Give no donations or support to AFL-CIO**.-This shows this Administration that we know who there right arm is. This is the labor unions.
>
> 12. **Buy no products made in China, no fruits and vegetables, no clothes, no parts, not even auto parts made in China**.-This will show this Administration that we the American people do not want to be borrowing any money from China. We would like good relations with China, but not at the cost of our Economy.

Now, you will notice some of these Embargos are in Italic type; these embargos are the most important of all. Try to do all of these embargos if you can. These embargos in Italic print will hurt the liberals most of all. The point of these embargos is to do something now, fight back now. Vote without waiting to vote. Telling this Administration that we do not like the way business in Washington is being conducted.